THE BASICS

2ND EDITION

European Union: The Basics is a clear and accessible introduction to the politics of the European Union, written by a leading authority in the field. This new edition has been fully updated and features extra material on the EU's global role as well as recent policies and rule changes. It covers topics such as:

- how the EU works and why it works this way
- the EU's development to date and its likely evolution
- the EU's biggest problems and controversies
- the Lisbon Treaty

Including suggestions for further reading, key learning points and a glossary of names and terms, this is the ideal guide for anyone wanting to learn more about the place and function of the European Union.

Alex Warleigh-Lack is Professor of Politics and International Relations at Brunel University, UK. He was Chair of UACES, the University Association for Contemporary European Studies, between 2006 and 2009, and has given policy advice to politicians, governments and research funders across Europe. He is editor of Understanding European Union Institutions, also published by Routledge.

The Basics

EUROPEAN UNION

THE BASICS

2ND EDITION

alex warleigh-lack

Routledge
Taylor & Francis Group

LONDON AND NEW YORK

First edition published 2004
Second edition, 2009
by Routledge
2 Park Square, Milton Park, Abingdon, Oxon OX14 4RN

Simultaneously published in the USA and Canada
by Routledge
711 Third Avenue, New York, NY 10017 (8th Floor)

Routledge is an imprint of the Taylor & Francis Group, an informa business

© 2004, 2009 Alex Warleigh-Lack

Typeset in Aldus and Scala by
Book Now Ltd, London
Printed and bound in Great Britain by
TJ International, Padstow, Cornwall

British Library Cataloguing in Publication Data
A catalogue record for this book is available from the British Library

Library of Congress Cataloging in Publication Data
Warleigh, Alex.
European Union: the basics/Alex Warleigh-Lack. — 2nd ed.
  p. cm.
Includes bibliographical references and index.
1. European Union. 2. European Union countries—Politics and government. I. Title.
JN30.W368 2008
341.242'2—dc22   2008010914

ISBN10: 0–415–41466–0 (hbk)
ISBN10: 0–415–41467–9 (pbk)
ISBN10: 0–203–89106–6 (ebk)

ISBN13: 978–0–415–41466–1 (hbk)
ISBN13: 978–0–415–41467–8 (pbk)
ISBN13: 978–0–203–89106–3 (ebk)

DEDICATION

This book is dedicated to everyone who fought for civil partnership legislation in the United Kingdom, in ways both large and small.

For Michael and Benedict – with great love

And last, but NEVER least, to my wonderful husband Christopher.

CONTENTS

PREFACE TO THE
SECOND EDITION

When the first edition of this book was written in 2003, the EU was entering a period of great uncertainty after the collapse of the process of negotiating a new Treaty. This period has lasted ever since, although the Treaty of Lisbon, agreed in December 2007 as this edition of the book was being finalised, may bring a successful conclusion to it. In those intervening years, much has happened to and in the EU, which has evolved from a Western European organisation to a pan-continental one, and seen heated debates not just about its policies, but about its legitimacy, its proper place in the world, and its internal workings. The 'basics' about the European Union have not altered beyond recognition since 2004; nonetheless, they are not quite the same as they were – hence the need for a second edition.

A feature of the first edition was its attempt to be both up-to-date and accessible; to judge by the feedback I have received from both my fellow academics and students (not all of them my own!), that goal was met pretty successfully. I hope that this second edition does the same. However, just as with the first edition, there are limits to how up-to-date a book such as this can be: even by the start of academic year 2008–9, much more will be known about the fate of the Treaty of Lisbon than can be established as I write. Thus, although Chapter 6 of the book includes a lengthy section on the Treaty of Lisbon and sets out how it is likely to impact on the EU if it is ratified, these changes are not fully integrated into the other chapters because they do not yet actually apply; given the demise of the Constitutional Treaty, it is not entirely safe to assume that they *will* apply, even if this is likely. So, if you are reading this book after the Treaty of Lisbon has been ratified across the EU, I suggest that you cross-reference Chapters 3 and 4, which set out the EU's institutions and policy-making processes, with Chapter 6, which discusses the Treaty of Lisbon in the context of other challenges and controversies on the EU agenda. If you are reading it after the Treaty collapses, I suggest you use Chapter 6 to think about why that has been the case. I suggest that you use the websites listed in Appendix I to make sure you have up-to-date information. A wonderful source of such information can also be found in the website of UACES, the University Association for Contemporary European Studies, which is the world's most dynamic EU studies association: www.uaces.org.

In addition to updates of all the existing chapters, this second edition includes a new Chapter 5 dedicated to the EU's external policies and activities, and a correspondingly altered Chapter 4, which now focuses on the EU's internal policies. Chapters 6 and 7 have been extensively re-written, and new scenarios for the EU's future are included in the latter.

I hope this book helps you understand the basics about the European Union, and to generate your own critical, informed view of it. That is the book's purpose, and if it is achieved it will be good compensation for the many weekends and evenings spent at the computer.

Professor Alex Warleigh-Lack
London, January 2008

BOXES
(KEY LEARNING POINTS)

ACKNOWLEDGEMENTS

I would like to thank Sage Publications for their permission to use material from my *Democracy in the EU: Theory Practice and Reform* in Chapter 2 of this book. The text has been substantially re-written here, but both the line of argument and the approach of sections of Chapter 2 are similar to those which I take in the Sage publication.

I would also like to thank Christopher Warleigh-Lack for his help in making the text more accessible and in suggesting items for inclusion in the glossary, in both the first and the second editions.

ABBREVIATIONS

BENELUX	Belgium, the Netherlands and Luxembourg
CAP	Common Agricultural Policy
CFI	Court of First Instance
CFSP	Common Foreign and Security Policy
COR	Committee of the Regions
COREPER	Committee of Permanent Representatives
DC	Draft Constitution
DG	Directorate General
EC	European Community
ECB	European Central Bank
ECHR	European Court of Human Rights *or* European Convention on Human Rights
ECJ	European Court of Justice
ECSC	European Coal and Steel Community
EDC	European Defence Community
EEC	European Economic Community
EFTA	European Free Trade Association
EMU	Economic and Monetary Union
EP	European Parliament
EESC	Economic and Social Committee
ESCB	European System of Central Banks
EU	European Union

EURATOM	European Atomic Energy Community
GDP	Gross Domestic Product
IGC	Intergovernmental Conference
MEP	Member of European Parliament
NAFTA	North American Free Trade Area
NATO	North Atlantic Treaty Organisation
OECD	Organisation for Economic Co-operation and Development
OSCE	Organisation for Security and Co-operation in Europe
QMV	Qualified Majority Voting
RRF	Rapid Reaction Force
SEA	Single European Act
SEM	Single European Market
TEU	Treaty on European Union
WTO	World Trade Organisation

INTRODUCTION

After more than fifty years, the politics of European integration still has the power to engross. The unique mixture of international organisation and **transnational polity** that is the European Union of today (EU, the Union) does not lend itself to easy classification in traditional academic categories. Moreover, the last two decades have seen an amazing rate of change in the structures, processes and competences of the EU. Indeed, since the Treaty on European Union (TEU) was signed at Maastricht in 1992 in the heady days of 'euro-phoria', four new Treaties on the workings of the Union have been agreed. One of them (the Constitutional Treaty) was rejected after negative referenda in France and the Netherlands in 2005, and, as this book is being written, the final Treaty in this flotilla, the Treaty of Lisbon, is going through the process of ratification in order to fill most of the gaps that were left by its stillborn predecessor.

What the EU does, and who it does this for, has also changed enormously in recent years. The Union has acquired its own currency (the euro), which as of January 2008 is in use in fifteen of the twenty-seven **member states**, and the beginnings of real cooperation in foreign and even defence policy. This adds an impressive range of new tasks to the Union's pre-existing competences in matters such as constructing and facilitating the **single European market** and agriculture. Since 1995, the Union has also welcomed, in three rounds of 'enlargement', new member states from Scandinavia, Central and Eastern Europe and the Mediterranean – with several countries still in the queue, for example, Croatia and Turkey. 'Europe', as many people continue rather vaguely to call the EU, has an impact on many issues of import across and beyond its member states. These issues range from the very technical, with a primary impact on a fairly narrow range of people (e.g. trading standards in particular goods), to vital issues of **macroeconomics** (the single currency) or environmental protection. European Union law gives member state nationals rights which they can invoke in their national courts, and is even, albeit on a basis that is subject to frequent contestation, supreme over any national law of the member states with which it conflicts.

For some observers, 'Europe' has become an interfering monster, a set of institutions bent on enhancing their own power by becoming involved in ever greater numbers of issues which would be better dealt with at national, regional or local level, or even left to the market to regulate. For others, the EU is too weak, a set of institutions which is obliged to find ways to reinforce itself where it can, rather than a 'proper state' with clear powers, its own resources, and a monopoly on legitimate power – at least in certain policy areas. As ever, the truth lies somewhere in the middle. The Union now has at least some role to play in the making of policy across a whole range of issues, but there are also clear limits to its powers. Moreover, this state of affairs has arisen rather more as a result of deliberate choices made by member state governments than as a consequence of power-grabbing by rapacious 'Brussels'. As is made clear in Chapter 3, despite the fact that actors from EU institutions other than the Council (which represents the member states), and even from outside the EU bodies entirely, can have a significant influence over the content of policy made by the Union, ultimately the national governments of the member states remain in charge. When it comes to designing the rules of the system, and deciding in what ways and in what areas the EU shall have competence, it is the member states which decide.[1] On matters of day-to-day legislation, member states share legislative power with the **European Parliament** in certain areas, but keep other policy areas almost completely to themselves. In other words, if the EU matters more in the lives of every citizen of its member states than in the past and is more powerful than any other international organisation, that is because the member states have chosen to allow this to happen.

Why have they done so? A detailed explanation of this issue is given in Chapter 2, but in order to help explain the approach taken in this book it makes sense to discuss the key parts of an answer to this query here. In essence, the EU's member states have used it as a means by which they can solve policy problems which would otherwise remain intractable, or which would at least not be addressed so effectively by individual member states on their own. These issues range from matters of post-**Second World War** economic recovery and guarantee of the food supply to matters of market regulation (the rather drier and more technical issues of supporting a suitable framework for economic growth, represented most clearly by the 'single European market' project) and even development policy (the provision of at least some co-ordination of member states' efforts to alleviate poverty in the so-called 'Third World').

The use of the EU as a tool in solving policy problems obviously demands a degree of mutual understanding, or at least a readiness to compromise, on the part of the member states. For some observers, this extends little further than mutual back-scratching: one member state may agree to let the EU act in one policy area, if another member state agrees to allow the Union to be active in another. For other observers, this represents the germ of a new way of 'doing politics' – it represents a kind of reflex of co-operation which makes collaboration with other member states a routine method for resolving policy problems. To some degree, this is a case of the old metaphor in which the glass can be seen as either half-full or half-empty. What is clear, however, is that over time the member states have used the EU more and more often as a means of solving policy problems. Thus, each member state has become 'Europeanised' (see Chapter 2) – that is, they have become part of a transnational system in which, within a limited if extensive number of policy areas, co-operation with other member states is necessary in order to produce public policy. Over the fifty or so years of European integration thus far, the EU has not replaced the member states. Instead, it has become 'fused' with them (Wessels 1997); via their membership of the EU, member states have developed new institutionalised links both with the Union and, via the institutions of the EU, with each other.

Just as clearly, however, the ways in which the member states seek to use the system of co-operation which they have created have changed over time. Initially, the aim was to give virtually all power to the Union in certain key areas of policy: this process was supposed eventually to lead to the birth of a new federal state, because one area of European cooperation would require support from another in order to work effectively – the idea of 'spillover'. For example, once coal and steel production became subject to joint control, the defence industries to which they made such key contributions would also be harmonised, leading to the need for common foreign and defence policies and thus a common European government. This was the so-called 'Monnet Method' of integration, named after **Jean Monnet**, one of the pioneers of European integration.

Over time, however, the Union has evolved into a very different kind of organisation. The spillover idea did not reach its full potential – certain member governments, most notably France, made it clear very early in the process of integration that they would not agree to an automatic transfer of power to the EU in policy areas they considered to be vital for their own national interest. Thus, for example, the proposed European Defence Community that would have followed hotfoot on the Economic and Steel Community failed to come into existence. As a result, the evolution of the EU has been much more complex, characterised by rather elliptical trajectories and tussles over the balance between national and European-level power; it has produced a situation in which the Union has far more power in certain areas of policy, especially trade and agriculture, than in others, e.g. tax.

Moreover, since the 1980s the neoliberal idea that the state (or international organisation/system) should do as little as possible, and leave the maximum possible room for manoeuvre to the market, has held sway in the EU almost as clearly as it has in many of the individual member states. Thus, when the Union acquires new competences now, it usually does so as a forum in which guidelines can be set, standards can be benchmarked, and good practice can be exchanged by means of the 'open method of coordination' (OMC). Such measures are, for example, the way in which the EU takes action against unemployment. In other words, the EU now acts more frequently as a co-ordination device which allows member states to develop their own respective approaches to common problems within an agreed framework than as a provider of detailed legislation which member states must then implement according to a preordained scheme.

GROWING PAINS: THE EUROPEAN UNION'S QUESTIONS SURPLUS

The undoubted expansion of EU competence has not, to put it mildly, made the Union any less controversial. Despite the fact that it now does more for its citizens than ever before,[2] and also the fact that it has a very 'light touch' when compared with the federalist approaches of its founders (see Chapter 2), the Union's perceived legitimacy is actually brought into question more regularly now than in the past. Its member states often differ bitterly about they think the EU should do, and how much power they are ultimately ready to cede to, or, in more EU-friendly language, 'pool in', the Union. Moreover, EU citizens frequently appear to find the notion of deepening integration at least as problematic now as in the past.

Thus, there is a paradox at the heart of European integration: the EU is now vastly more important to the lives of all who live in its member states than at its creation, and yet this growth in importance has not necessarily increased the Union's popularity. Nor has the EU become part of the conscious 'lived experience' of most of its citizens, who continue to be, on the whole, unaware of both the EU's powers and its limits. This is particularly obvious in states such as the UK, where Euro-myths about straight bananas and the like tend to be all that most citizens hear about on the subject of the EU, whose single market legislation in fact helps make their daily lives more varied (you would not find houmous in Sainsbury's in the 1950s), and whose freedom of personal movement rights make it easy for rain-lashed Brits (and Dutch, and Germans…) to buy up vast stretches of sunnier member states or just take holidays there. However, it is also true of member states whose citizens tend to be less sceptical about the Union – such as in Spain.

A further complication makes the issues facing the EU become even more daunting. The recent **enlargement** of the EU to many countries of the former Soviet bloc and the micro-states of Malta and Cyprus has made the Union a truly continental system. Indeed it has made the Union the world's biggest market by quite some way. It has also made the EU far more diverse, in terms of the relative wealth and political culture of its member states, and the policy preferences of national elites. Thus, the Union will have to make good on its long-held ambition to achieve 'unity in diversity'. It will also have to reinvent itself, moving away from its period as a club of fairly homogeneous West European states towards a future as a structure which is capable of providing (or at least co-ordinating) much of the public policy making of most of the continent. Such a process requires mutual adaptation between states from the East and West, as well as the North and South, of the continent, and has so far sometimes proved problematic. Western European states – notably France – have often been rather *de haut en bas* with their Eastern European partners; in return, the latter have often seen the EU as too politically progressive by half, particularly regarding secularism and the treatment of ethnic minorities/lesbian, gay, bisexual and transgender issues. An example is Poland.

The idea that the EU, or its predecessors the European Economic Community and the European Community, is at a vital crossroads where crucial decisions about its future impose themselves is not new. Indeed, it has long been something of a cliché, and many observers of the Union have regularly wondered how it continues to function in its rather idiosyncratic manner. If it is ratified, the Treaty of Lisbon may provide some answers, but even this document will not on its own make the EU even more capable of powerful action on key policy challenges such as climate change. This is because such issues are really only partly about institutions and decision-making rules, i.e. the kind of thing to be found in the EU's treaties. Instead, they are also about the ideas, values and interests which shape national governments' decisions about the changes to the EU system and range of EU policies that they are willing to accept.

The EU continues to face many challenges, some internal, some external (as discussed in Chapter 6). The ability to provide, or at least help provide, environmental and energy security is an obvious example, as is the ability to address international migration. After the collapse of the Constitutional Treaty in 2005, the EU may now be emerging from a period of introspection; this certainly appears to be the wish of most national governments, who hope the Treaty of Lisbon will be ratified and endure for some time, meaning issues of institutional reform will fall right to the bottom of the EU agenda. However, at the time of writing, this cannot be taken for granted, and consequently the Union may only have postponed the need to ask and answer some very pointed questions about its future. Should, or can, the EU become a federal state, a continental power capable of rivalling the USA and provide an alternative patron in the global political economy to weaker **third countries**? Can the process of European integration be deepened without going down the road to federalism? Has European integration already gone too far – and if so, can, or should, it be 'rolled back' so that its member states can once again be more truly autonomous? How should the EU relate to other organisations with a role in European governance, such as **NATO**, or the **Council of Europe**? Should it aim to replace, or co-operate with, them? And how should the EU relate to, and perhaps work with, those states which are either unwilling to join, or incapable of joining, the Union? Perhaps most importantly of all, what can the EU do if its member states – and their peoples – take different views about all these issues? Currently, then, the EU suffers from a surplus of questions about its own role and future, and a deficit of answers.

HOW TO USE THIS BOOK

Aids to understanding

This book thus seeks to help the reader find his or her own ways to reduce the EU's question surplus. It is aimed at either the 'intelligent layperson', who requires a solid introduction to the EU for professional or general informational purposes, or the non-specialist/beginner student who needs a good introduction to the key issues on the EU agenda, grounded in an understanding of how and why the EU has developed to its current condition. The book is thus, I hope, written in accessible language. However, the book also retains academic conventions and style so that those who so choose can use it as a platform to further study of the EU.

The book has several features which are designed to aid comprehension and facilitate further learning. Each chapter after this Introduction includes key learning points, which help the reader focus on the most salient of the issues addressed. Each chapter also contains think points which, while not necessarily designed as essay questions, certainly help the reader both focus on key issues and reflect on them. The chapter on the EU's history begins with a timeline of the most important events in the EU's development to date. I also include in each chapter a brief guide to further reading – up to six particularly useful texts which allow the interested reader to explore the academic literature on the pertinent issues in more depth. At the end of the book is a glossary of key terms used, including theoretical concepts and acronyms. The book also has two appendices. The first consists of a list of websites which can provide further information about, or analysis of, the politics of European integration. The second is a list of member states as of January 2008.

Themes and objectives

The book has two key themes. First, I argue that the current politics of European integration cannot be understood without reference to the following factors:

- historical trends, i.e. the concept of 'path dependence'. This is the idea that events/decisions which were made previously have an important impact on decisions made in the present day, either by restricting the range of possible options or by shaping perceptions held by key people of what should be done about a given problem.
- pressures from global, or at least international, systems and processes. Without the decision of the USA to support and fund (West) European integration after the Second World War, for example, there is every reason to doubt that the EU would exist in its present form.
- pressures from domestic politics. Which problems either cannot be solved by a member state of the EU acting independently, or might be solved more effectively through partnership with other member states? How far, and why, are citizens and governments in the member states willing to support the European integration process?
- the role of ideas and beliefs, as well as national (and EU institutions' own) interests, in shaping what actors involved with the integration process want to achieve. In other words, we cannot understand the outcomes of the European integration process merely by looking at what we, as observers, think has been the 'national interest' set out by a given member state government. Instead, we need to understand how beliefs and values – about the integration process itself, the kind of policies it should encompass

and the actual content of those policies – shape what the EU is able to do. For example, it is perfectly possible that member states should agree that the EU should help ensure each member state has low inflation. Indeed, this is the key role of the European Central Bank (see Chapter 2). However, some member states consider that this objective can best be achieved by membership of the single currency, the euro; others prefer to remain outside the euro, and pursue the goal of low inflation by means they choose themselves. At the time of writing, Slovenia falls into the first category, but the United Kingdom falls into the second.

As a second theme, I argue that the European integration process has produced not a federal state but rather an idiosyncratic, if often extremely tightly-bound, political system. I argue that this system was established when the original six member states began to co-operate over the production of coal and steel, which were then key sectors of the economy. It has since been shaped into a novel kind of compromise between those whose ambition was to create a 'United States of Europe', and those who wished to use European integration more instrumentally, that is, as a tool to adopt in order to meet a specific objective, without creating an entity capable of replacing its member states.

In order to explore these arguments, I set out four key objectives.

- First, to explain both how the EU works – how it produces public policy and legislation – and why it works in the particular fashion it has adopted.
- Second, to set out and explain the EU's most important policies and achievements.
- Third, to set out and discuss the most important issues and problems currently on the EU agenda.
- Fourth, to provide the means by which the reader can generate her or his own informed understanding about the EU's likely development in the coming years.

Structure of the book

The book breaks down into the following structure. Chapter 2 explores the history of European integration from the late 1940s to the present day. It explains why the EU's development has often been slow and contested but has nonetheless failed to reach either a dead-end (stagnation) or the outcome desired by many of its supporters (a new federal United States of Europe). I argue that the EU has developed as a means by which the (West) European state has been able to adapt in the face of key challenges such as the rise of the **welfare state**, economic interdependence and the need to ensure that the devastation of the Second World War was not repeated. Within this broad agreement that co-operation is useful, each of the member states has different objectives to be secured from the integration process. The condition of the integration process – and indeed the content of any of its policies – thus reflects the nature of the agreement that can be forged among the member states and, in day-to-day policy making, the EU institutions, at any given time.

Chapter 3 explores the institutions and decision-making processes of the EU. It sets out the roles and functions of the EU's major institutions, and explains not just what they do, but how they do it. The structure of the EU is explained, as is the EU's innovative and unique legal system. Crucially, the chapter also shows how – at least for the strictly 'political' institutions – coalition building is the key to success. In other words, although the EU has several major institutions, and different ways of sharing out power between them depending on the issue at hand, it is vital to remember that in EU politics no single member state or institution is all-powerful.

Chapter 4 sets out and evaluates the EU's major internal policies. It explores the single market, the single currency, the Common Agricultural Policy, regional policy and environment policy. The chapter sets out the rationales behind each policy, and explains why and to what extent the EU has power in that area. I explore why and to what extent the EU's powers vary according to the policy area in question, and why this balance has changed over time. The main factors examined to explain this variation are the concept of **national sovereignty**, the EU budget, **globalisation** and **neoliberalism**.

Chapter 5 carries out a similar function for the EU's external policies – external trade and economic diplomacy, security and defence matters and development policy. I argue in this chapter that the EU is an increasingly important shaper of world events, albeit one with rather obvious limits, and that it therefore acts as a significant complement to member states' own individual foreign policies.

Chapter 6 examines problematic issues of the EU agenda in terms of the proverbial 'big picture'. Here, I concentrate on issues of governance (democracy, the division of power between member states and the EU, the role of 'opting out'), Euroscepticism, enlargement, and the EU budget. I also focus on the Treaty of Lisbon, paying particular attention to how this will change the EU system if it is ratified. The purpose of the chapter is to explain why these issues are so inherently problematic, and how they are often inter-linked.

Chapter 7 is the final section of the book. I here provide a summary of the major points covered in the book, and then use concepts from integration theory to set out different visions of the way in which the EU might develop in the coming years. These 'visions' are not predictions. Rather, they give the reader an overview of some key schools of thought in integration theory, covering both how they explain the development of the EU so far and what they expect of the EU's future evolution. This chapter therefore aims to set the issues covered in the rest of the book in theoretical context and to allow those who wish to undertake further reading/study to do so in a theoretically-informed way.

THE EVOLUTION OF EUROPEAN INTEGRATION

INTRODUCTION

The purpose of this chapter is to provide answers to three essential questions. First, how has the EU evolved? Second, why has it had this particular developmental trajectory? And third, how can the current stage in the EU's evolution be characterised? The argument of the chapter is that the EU's development has been indelibly marked by conflict and difficult collaboration, but has nonetheless reached the point at which it constitutes a novel transnational polity. This polity has been meshed, or 'fused' (Wessels 1997) with its member states, and has not replaced them. This is largely because the EU has been primarily viewed by its member states as a tool to be used in solving otherwise intractable problems rather than as the product of idealism. Thus, the increasing recourse to the EU as a device for the making of public policy has provoked the '**Europeanisation**' of the member states. In has locked them together, both vertically (with the EU structures and processes) and horizontally (with each other). The chapter is structured in three parts, with a section devoted to each of the three questions raised above.

THE EVOLUTION OF THE EUROPEAN UNION: A TIMELINE

In order to chart the development of the EU, it is useful to set out some of the key events in the Union's life to date. The following timeline is not an exhaustive list; instead, it takes into account major institutional and membership changes, including several key rulings by the European Court of Justice. A discussion of the events included in the timeline then follows.

Year	Event
1951	European Coal and Steel Community (ECSC) established by Treaty of Paris, beginning a new phase in post-Second World War European integration process. Member states are France, Germany, Italy and **Benelux**.
1954	European Defence Community (EDC) fails to be established – integration process is set back.
1957	European Economic Community (EEC) and European Atomic Energy Community (Euratom) are established by Treaty of Rome, reviving the integration process.
1959	European Free Trade Association (**EFTA**) established by the UK as a rival to the EEC.
1963	European Court of Justice (ECJ) rules in *Van Gend en Loos* that member state nationals can invoke EC law directly before national courts – the principle of 'direct effect'.
1964	ECJ rules in *Costa* that EC law is supreme over any national law with which it conflicts – the 'supremacy' principle.
1965	'Empty chair crisis' provoked by France; resolved by agreement to reassert national veto power and avoid giving more power to the EU's institutions (the so-called 'Luxembourg Agreement').
1965	Merger Treaty (officially merges the institutions of the ECSC, EEC and Euratom).
1965–1985	'Eurosclerosis' – relative stagnation of the integration process, the result of the empty chair crisis.
1973	First enlargement of the EEC (to Denmark, Ireland and the UK); EFTA no longer a credible rival.
1979	First direct elections to the European Parliament; rejection by the new Parliament of the EEC budget as demonstration of its will to use its powers.

1979	ECJ rules in *Cassis-de-Dijon* that EEC market can be based on agreed minimum standards rather than harmonisation.
1980	Second enlargement of the EEC (to Greece).
1986	Third enlargement of the EEC (to Portugal and Spain).
1986	**Single European Act** continues process of revival of European integration, bringing in the title of 'European Community' and establishing the single European market.
1989	Collapse of **Communism** in Central and Eastern Europe. Has major impact on direction and process of European integration.
1991	ECJ rules in *Francovich* that member states can be penalised for non-implementation, or inadequate implementation, of EC law – the principle of 'state liability'.
1992	Treaty on European Union (TEU) agreed at Maastricht. Takes the integration process much closer to the achievement of a European **federation**, and re-names the EC the 'European Union'.
1992	Danes reject the TEU in their first referendum on it, and crisis of '**democratic deficit**' begins in earnest.
1995	Fourth enlargement of the EU (to Austria, Finland and Sweden).
1997	Treaty of Amsterdam makes cautious, limited additions to the EU treaties.
1997	German Constitutional Court pronounces in *Brunner* that the ECJ does not have 'kompetenz-kompetenz', i.e. the ECJ cannot decide when national sovereignty is broached.
1999	**European Commission** resigns in face of alleged maladministration.
2000	Treaty of Nice is agreed. It makes very little contribution to the process of EU reform, but establishes institutional basis for further enlargement. Initially rejected by a referendum in Ireland, the Treaty is ratified eventually in 2002.
2002	The single currency, the euro, is launched successfully. Twelve member states take part.

2002	**Convention on the Future of Europe** is established.
2003	Convention produces Draft Constitutional Treaty, which the member states fail to accept.
2004	Fifth enlargement of the EU (to Cyprus, the Czech Republic, Estonia, Hungary, Latvia, Lithuania, Malta, Poland, Slovakia and Slovenia).
2004	A revised Constitutional Treaty is agreed by the member states.
2005	Constitutional Treaty rejected after France and the Netherlands vote against it in referenda; EU plunges into constitutional crisis.
2007	Sixth enlargement of the EU (to Bulgaria and Romania).
2007	Treaty of Lisbon agreed by member states to replace the failed Constitutional Treaty.

A BRIEF HISTORY OF THE EUROPEAN UNION: ACCOUNTING FOR DIFFICULT EVOLUTION

Recovering from the Second World War: dependence on the USA, and the search for autonomy

To understand the reasons for the establishment of the EU, it is necessary to investigate the history of Europe in the early to mid-twentieth century. To some extent, this is because of the obvious and usual rationale given for the justification of the EU, namely that it prevented the outbreak of war between countries which had twice brought each other to the brink of destruction in the 30 years or so between 1914 and 1945. However, this investigation is also necessary for another reason: to understand the changing role of the European state, and the increase and change in the responsibilities with which it was entrusted. Preserving the peace was undoubtedly part of the rationale for the EU's creation; but the changing expectations placed on European states, and their need to mutate in order to satisfy those expectations, was also crucial.

The tasks of government in Europe increased enormously as a response to the Great Depression of the 1920s, itself in large part a

> ## BOX 2.1: KEY LEARNING POINT –
> ## THE IMPORTANCE OF HISTORY
>
> Historical factors are very important in explaining the creation and evolution of the EU. First, there is the need to understand the specific historical context in which European integration began – the end of the Second World War, the resultant dominance of the USA and the USSR (the 'superpowers'), and the corresponding weakness of the European countries. Second, there is the need to understand the historical legacy in terms of changing demands upon governments in the early twentieth century – citizens increasingly wanted their governments to produce services and goods for them in order to receive support, but it was by no means clear how such extensive state structures could be built in war-torn Europe. Third, there is a need to understand the EU's own history, which has been one of evolution-through-argument. This history has shaped what citizens and politicians expect from it, both positively and negatively (see Kaiser and Starie 2005).

product of the First World War. As argued by Hobsbawm (1994), there was a clear attack on nineteenth century traditions of **laissez-faire** minimalism. Left-wing politicians were drawn to ideas of communism and socialism, arguing that the state had a duty to ensure the well-being of its poorest citizens. Socialist and communist parties were formed across Europe, acting as focal points for the many who were disadvantaged by the existing regimes. Parties of the extreme right also grew in response to a perceived communist threat, especially after the bloody Russian Revolution of 1917. These parties often sought to defend 'traditional' values against erosion. Nonetheless, they too sought to strengthen the state in order to ensure that their power could be used effectively, and buy the citizens' loyalty through providing **public goods**.

When European governance structures were being re-built after the Second World War, this had to be done in a very difficult set of circumstances. Citizens still expected states to be providing them with clear benefits in order to win their support. However, the war had greatly reduced European states' ability to do this, because it had devastated the European economy and caused all European countries – even the supposedly victorious United Kingdom – to lose their 'Great Power' status. Indeed, the two new superpowers of the world (the United States and the **Soviet Union**, or USSR) literally divided Europe between them at the **Yalta** summit of 1945. Crudely put, the USA retained control over the Western part of the continent, and the USSR was granted its own sphere of influence in the East. Thus, the states seeking to re-establish themselves in Western Europe had to do so whilst accepting the following conditions:

- US dominance, both economically and militarily;
- reduced economic capacity;
- the loss of 'great power' status and, slowly, their remaining colonies;
- the perceived need to defend themselves against potential subversion by Communists (or even, in some cases, invasion by the USSR);
- the need to justify their existence to citizens by preserving peace, and guaranteeing basic welfare and food provision.

In sum, the sheer scale of the challenges facing European leaders was enormous, and co-operation was clearly required if they were to be met. Moreover, the post-war leader of the West, the USA, made it clear that it was prepared to donate both economic aid and military protection only if its new client states were prepared to work together rather than oppose each other. In this situation, it is worth explaining why Europe's politicians did not simply build a European federation. After all, the construction of such structures was a time-honoured means to ensure that states facing extreme challenges, either internally or externally, sought strength by building strong alliances with each other, thereby both avoiding war and enabling efforts to be concentrated on economic development (Forsyth 1981).

In fact, there was no sustained pressure for the creation of a European federation from any of the key actors: the prevailing superpowers, the leaders of post-war Western Europe, and the citizens of the continent.[1]

First, there was insufficient pressure from the most powerful states which held a stake in European stability in the immediate post-war world: the USA, the USSR and (at least for a short time) the UK. Neither of the then superpowers consistently sought to establish a European federation. The US was not necessarily opposed to the idea, and indeed many important actors in the US foreign policy community considered that it was the logical choice for a continent in need of economic integration as well as guaranteed peace (Dinan 1999:17). However, although the USA offered much-needed financial aid to the European states through the 1947 **Marshall Plan**, and insisted that the recipient states must co-operate in its implementation, it did not insist on the creation of a United States of Europe in the face of opposition from the two most powerful West European states of the day – the UK and France (Hobsbawm 1994). Instead, as a central plank of its strategy for post-war pre-eminence, **Cold War** diplomacy and greater prosperity, the USA gave its support to other forms of European co-operation in which it played an official role as participant rather than merely sponsor, and indeed, in the case of NATO, clearly as first among equals.

The USSR perceived no interest in a post-war European federation, above all because the latter was seen to be a covert means by which the USA could, if permitted, extend its influence into countries included in the Soviet sphere of influence at Yalta. Worse, even if confined to the Western half of the continent, integration could set up a potential rival power to the USSR. The strong security rationale for this opposition – the insistence on the division of Germany, the creation of a *cordon sanitaire,* and the control of neighbouring countries which had often caused problems for Russian/Soviet security (Dawisha 1990) – was coupled with an ideological equivalent. Most of the nominally autonomous countries of Central and Eastern Europe had very little independence as part of the USSR's empire-cum-buffer-zone.[2] However, it is also true that successive leaders of the USSR derived part of their domestic legitimacy from claims to be at the head of a group of nations which would be the vanguard of a new communist world order (Dawisha 1990:11).[3] Thus, the Soviet Union had little to gain from supporting the idea of European federalism, although as the Cold War deepened, the USSR can be said to have contributed indirectly to European integration in the Western half of the continent by providing an enemy against whom it was considered necessary to unite under the protection of the USA. By the same token, the USSR came to accept the integration process as part of the status quo which enabled it to dominate its half of Europe whilst the superpowers played out their conflict in other arenas of the globe.

Despite much pro-integration rhetoric from its war-time leader Winston Churchill, the United Kingdom was at best ambivalent about the desirability of such an entity as a federal European state (Young 1998). For most UK politicians at the close of the Second World War, European integration in matters other than free trade had symbolic importance but was unlikely to succeed; federation was certainly a project in which the UK could have no role given the required sacrifice of national sovereignty. Ultimately, however, the integration project was to be encouraged if it made 'the continent' stable and thereby allowed the UK to achieve strategic importance as the crucial link between the USA, the **Commonwealth** and Europe. Britain's reluctant accession to the EU in 1973 owes as much to an admission that it had miscalculated the integration process' possibilities for success as to an exaggeration of the UK's ability to remain prosperous on the outside.[4]

A second, and perhaps even more crucial, factor was that those states which participated in the post-war European institutions, and even those which agreed to join the predecessor of the EU, the European Coal and Steel Community of 1952, did so primarily as a means of securing the national interest rather than out of federalist zeal (Milward 1992; Moravcsik 1999). During the Second World War, bolstered by both left-wing ideas of internationalism and hard-learned lessons about the dangers of extreme nationalism, the popularity of federalism grew; many of those in war-time resistance movements in several countries had very strong attachments to the idea of a European federation as the means to resuscitate the continent (Urwin 1992: 7). However, not many of those who had been active in the wartime resistance movements became leaders of their countries after the war ended. Instead, with the uniting strand of a struggle against a common enemy dissolved, the internally diverse resistance movements splintered and the reins of power were often taken up either by former leaders returning from exile or those under their tutelage. These actors' views on integration were far more instrumental, and less idealistic, than those of participants in the Resistance (Urwin 1992: 7–12).

The third factor was that there was no clamouring for a European federation at popular level which could have provided the basis for a bold leader or set of leaders to seize the day. In addition to the dissipation of the Resistance and its pro-federal loyalties, there was the deliberate re-focusing of the popular imagination on the idea and structure of the nation state by national elites (Milward 1992; Weigall and Stirk 1992). Thus, federalists had relatively little support on which to draw, and most of those in positions of power routinely opposed their ideas about the shape European integration should take, even if they supported other forms of European co-operation.

The Monnet Strategy: the 'domino approach' to European integration and a new 'path dependency'

Given the absence of support for federalism, those concerned to promote European integration had to seek out other means. A key figure here is Jean Monnet, who was to become the first President of the High Authority of the European Coal and Steel Community (ECSC) and who consistently pushed a sort of 'domino theory' of European integration which came to acquire the support of the main politicians in France and Germany. This approach to European co-operation held that a federation could be built gradually, by working in first one sector of policy and then moving on to others as Europeans got used to the idea of collaboration with each other and also realised that co-operation in any given sector, or part of a sector, could only work effectively if the other policy areas to which it was linked also became subject to collaboration at European level. This approach thus saw European integration to be rather like so many dominoes lined up on their edges; knocking the first of them over would eventually bring all the others down too.

BOX 2.2: KEY LEARNING POINT – THE 'MONNET METHOD'

The method of integration devised by Jean Monnet is vital to understand for two reasons. First, it was perhaps the only means by which European integration could be accepted by the member states (starting with areas of economic policy, and proceeding gradually, sector by sector, rather than in great leaps forward). Second, it has contributed not only to the successes of the EU but also to its failures and problems. The Monnet Method essentially placed great emphasis on a particular kind of rationality, namely that member states would prefer to maximise the gains they received from integration by allowing it to proceed from one area of policy to another, over their national autonomy. This assumption was not entirely correct; although the EU has developed almost beyond recognition since the 1950s, the pace of this growth has been dictated by the member states of the EU according to their collective agreement rather than by the 'objectively logical' steps that might be necessary to optimise gains from previous collaboration. The Monnet method also established the EU as an elite, rather than a democratic, organisation. It is therefore partly to blame for the 'democratic deficit' of the Union (see Bellamy and Warleigh 1998).

This strategy was, at first, very successful. Six states (France, Germany, Italy, Belgium, the Netherlands and Luxembourg) joined the ECSC in 1951. Monnet's approach allowed European politicians to co-operate in areas where they could see that benefits would be probable, but also to limit the amount of independence ('sovereignty') that they would have to sacrifice as part of the deal. Thus, there was something of a gamble made right at the start of the European integration process: Monnet and his supporters wagered that, once begun in given policy sectors, European integration would eventually prove unstoppable. Many national politicians bet on precisely the opposite outcome, namely that European integration could effectively be limited to certain sectors of their choosing. The history of what is now the EU indicates that, although many more areas of policy are now part of the EU's competence, it was national politicians who won the bet. In essence, this is because they were as alive to the potential 'domino effect' of **sectoral co-operation** as Monnet himself. As a result, they have continued to police the integration process very carefully, and have periodically either virtually abandoned it (during the 1970s), or made it clear that they would remain in control even when they gave the EU new powers. An example is the Treaty on European Union, which gave the EU competence in foreign and security policy, but both restricted this competence and ensured that national governments, not the EU institutions, remained in control of EU policy in this area.

The limits of the Monnet approach became clear very quickly. Although six national governments agreed to form the ECSC in 1951, the proposal to move from that to a European Defence Community failed in 1954: it was rejected by the French Parliament, and thus was not capable of being ratified. To a certain extent, the creation of such a community would have been logical: coal and steel were at the time the heart of not only economic regeneration but also military equipment (except, of course, for chemical and nuclear weapons, over which the superpowers then had a virtual monopoly). However, the member states simply were not ready either to trust each other enough to collaborate in matters of such importance, or to sacrifice (as they saw it) their independence in such crucial areas. Instead, after three more years, a further Treaty was signed to set up the European Economic Community (EEC) and the European Atomic Energy Community (Euratom). This was for two reasons. First, for those pushing the domino theory line, a switch of focus from coal to nuclear power was in keeping with then-apparent trends in energy production, and thus military capacity (Dinan 1999). Second, for all those concerned with economic growth – which included the member governments – the ideas that a common tariff could be applied between member states, and a common approach to the outside world could be adopted, was appealing.

This pattern has generally characterised the EU ever since. Thus, although co-operation in defence policy was more than a step too far, collaboration in broader sections of economic policy was of likely benefit and relatively little cost. That this kind of calculation was made seems even more apparent when the total outstripping of Euratom by the EEC is remembered.

Nonetheless, the Monnet method of European integration did succeed in locking the Union into an evolutionary pathway, deepening existing networks of actors and creating new ones to bolster the process (Kaiser and Starie 2005). On this path, the decisions made at any one time have to a great extent been shaped by previous decisions that had either created the institutions and processes of decision making or presented opportunities/problems which subsequently required action. This is not to suggest that politicians became powerless as a result of their own, or their predecessors', decisions. It is simply to maintain that agendas are often set, and beliefs about appropriate action conditioned by, previous actions (Hall and Taylor

1996). In terms of European integration, perhaps the main evidence of this is the belief of many – including officials of the EU institutions and national governments – that European integration is a battle for supremacy between EU and national levels, with the ultimate goal being either to create, or resist, a federal United States of Europe.

Empty chairs and eurosclerosis: apparent stagnation from 1965 to 1985

Such 'resistance' thinking was surely behind the actions of General **Charles de Gaulle**, President of France between 1958 and 1969. During that period he ensured that the then-EEC would not develop into a European federation, or anything like it. He resisted several attempts to expand the EEC to take in the UK and other states; he resisted attempts to add to the powers of the EU's institutions; and he resisted attempts to add new areas to the set of competences held at 'European' level.

De Gaulle's actions had their roots in a deep desire to preserve and promote French power. For de Gaulle, the EEC and its fellow 'communities' were useful to the degree that they enhanced French status and influence, particularly vis-à-vis Germany and the USA, or at least advanced key policy interests of the French republic, such as support for France's agricultural sector. However, should the EEC or any other 'European' institution show tendencies towards self-aggrandisement, or propose activity in either an area or a fashion not to the advantage of France, then for de Gaulle that should clearly be opposed (Balme and Woll 2005).

The General's logic led him to propose a European Security Community, which would have provided a framework of European security institutions to serve as a kind of overarching structure for European integration, which could then be confined to workaday and rather technical issues (Dinan 1999). These institutions, which would have been **intergovernmental** rather than federal, would have rivalled NATO, and thus reduced French (and, by extension, other member states') security dependence on the USA. At one level, this was an astonishing proposal for de Gaulle to make; it would certainly have integrated 'Europe' much more closely towards a common foreign and security policy than the Union has achieved even now. However, it did not please those devoted to the Monnet method, because

BOX 2.3: KEY LEARNING POINT – THE CONCEPT OF 'NATIONAL SOVEREIGNTY'

National sovereignty essentially means the ability of a state to decide on its own independent course of action, with no external force or other country able to impose their own preferences on what members of that nation (or at least the national elites) want to do. Although there are few, if any, examples of complete national sovereignty, because treaties, international laws and alliances can limit it formally, and the weaknesses of any given state can limit it in practice by opening up the possibility for foreign domination, it has been the guiding principle of political organisation in Europe since the seventeenth century. It remains a very important factor, both emotionally and practically, in European politics today. The relationship between national sovereignty and the EU is very important for two reasons. First, several member states' desire to preserve as much of their sovereignty – or independence – as possible has prevented the development of a federal United States of Europe. Second, however, the complexities and achievements of the EU mean that its member states in practice share sovereignty with each other and with the EU itself far more than is the case for other states in the world system. In this respect, the EU has actually been seen as the major case of 'post-sovereign' politics in a world where countries are deeply interdependent rather than separated from each other.

de Gaulle's plans would have sidelined the existing EEC structures and institutions. Moreover, other actors had concerns about the ambition to move away from dependence upon the USA (which dependence is often called '**Atlanticism**'). As a result, the General's proposals came to nothing despite an initial agreement in its favour between France and Germany – the Elysée Treaty of 1963.

Consequently, de Gaulle's approach to European integration was sceptical, and even combative. When the European Commission proposed a new budgetary regime, which would have given more power both to itself and to the European Parliament, instituted **qualified majority voting** in the **Council of Ministers**, and given the EEC an amount of its 'own resources' (collected through import levies) to fund the Common Agricultural Policy, de Gaulle refused to accept these proposals, and simply withdrew French representation in EEC meetings. The resultant 'empty chair' crisis brought the EEC to a virtual standstill, because unanimity was required for decisions in Council, and if France was not represented it could not vote. The crisis was eventually solved by the so-called Luxembourg compromise, which effectively ruled out qualified majority voting and made it clear that power would reside with the member states, via the Council. Business resumed; however, the Commission entered its own period of crisis, having received crystal clear signals that expansionist plans for either itself or the EEC as a whole would not be tolerated – at least while de Gaulle held power in what was then the most important member state, France.

As Cini (2002, 48–9) argues, the subsequent years were something of a low ebb in European integration. The Commission did not feel able – or was not permitted – to bring forward radical proposals for change, and upon completion of the major goal of the EEC (the **customs union**) in 1968, there was little to guide those seeking further European integration about which areas of policy to choose next, or how to go about them. When the 1970s brought economic crisis to Western Europe, the member states chose to attempt national solutions to common problems rather than joint activity via the EEC. Indeed, during the 1970s, a major European integration project – monetary union – failed. It seemed that European integration had reached its limits (Taylor 1983); although three new member states joined in 1973, and the European Parliament enjoyed its first set of direct elections in 1979, the EEC appeared virtually moribund to most political actors and commentators. In fact, however, this was not entirely the case. European Community law was used, to some extent, to push the process of European integration further than was possible through strictly political means (Weiler 1991; see also the above timeline for references to key judgements). Additional member states signed up to the integration process in 1980 (Greece), and 1986 (Spain and Portugal). Furthermore, pro-integration actors were gradually re-building their strength, re-building their networks, and looking for the right opportunity to make their case. This opportunity presented itself in the early to mid-1980s, and centred on the drive to create the 'single European market'.

From single market to European Union

The economic crises of the 1970s, which had initially tempted the member states to revert to 'beggar-my-neighbour' tactics in order to survive, ultimately caused deeper European integration. Through their very persistence, they required new kinds of action if they were to be resolved. According to Dinan (1999: 93–101), three key factors helped create and harness opinion in favour of establishing a 'single European market', which had long been a goal of the EEC but which had never been realised. The first was the ascendancy of neoliberalism – the idea that markets are better determiners and providers of public policy and wealth than governments, and thus markets should be as large, and as unconstrained, as possible. The second factor was the increase in transatlantic tension over economic priorities – West European companies became persuaded that without a single European market which discriminated in their favour against American and Asian rivals, they would never be competitive. The third factor was the Draft Treaty on European Union that was put forward by the European Parliament, which was concerned that European integration was floundering just at the time when economic problems in the member states called for its re-launch. Although the Draft Treaty was never ratified by the member states, it served to generate a debate and to reinforce the more eager member states (ironically by now including France) in their desire for progress.

Thus, a proverbial window of opportunity was opened. The idea of creating a single European market was one around which a broad coalition of support could be gathered. The ever-cautious British, under Margaret Thatcher, liked the idea of an even and open economic playing field for 'Europe', as did much of the European business community. They also considered that it would continue the earlier pattern of limiting integration to areas of economics, rather than tax, justice, foreign policy or defence. Integrationists liked the idea of realising an old objective of the EEC, and considered that it might well have 'spillovers' into other areas of policy. The European Court of Justice, intentionally or otherwise, had facilitated the single market initiative through its 1979 ruling in the *Cassis-de-Dijon* case (which effectively meant that a single market did not have to be founded on complete harmonisation of every product and sector – a mammoth and probably impossible task – but could instead be based on a set of agreed minimum standards for each sector/product). Furthermore, the then President of the Commission, **Jacques Delors**, was an effective and personable politician, who was able to harness this grand coalition of support and essentially maintain it until the necessary legislation was agreed.

Delors' achievement should not be underestimated. It is true that he was not acting alone, and it is also true that he chose to be active in a policy area in which national politicians were prepared to make progress in integration (Moravcsik 1991). However, Delors' skill in brokering the Single European Act (which established the single market) was impressive, for he managed to secure agreement on certain key issues of institutional design which had dogged the integration process since the days of de Gaulle. These centred on the role of the European Parliament, and the issue of qualified majority voting in the Council of Ministers. In order to make sure they achieved their objective of a single European market, the member states were prepared to both abandon their veto power (for issues relating to the single market), and to grant the European Parliament a second reading of legislative proposals – the so-called 'co-operation procedure'.[5]

Thus, in the mid-1980s, there was a significant 'recasting (of) the European bargain' (Sandholtz and Zysman 1989). This trend continued with the Treaty on European Union (TEU), signed at Maastricht in 1992. The TEU built on the successes of the Single European Act, and greatly expanded both the role and functions of what it called the 'European Union'. This was largely the result of two factors. First, the perceived need to maximise the benefits of the single market by introducing a common European currency. Second, the collapse of communism in Central and Eastern Europe, which itself had three major consequences: the reunification of Germany, the end of the Soviet Union as a perceived threat to Western Europe, and the need for Western Europe to develop the capacity to deal with the suddenly 'liberated' countries of the former Soviet bloc.

When communism collapsed in Eastern and Central Europe, the event took both Western Europeans and the USA by surprise. Moreover, it threatened to create chaos on the European continent: despite the fact that nobody actively liked the Cold War between the USA and its allies and the Soviet Union and its acolytes, it had become an established feature of European governance. It was, in a sense, the central fact around which all else was organised. With the collapse of both the USSR and its satellite regimes, Europe had to redefine what it means to be 'European'. It also had to create ways of managing the fact that it immediately became of less strategic interest to the USA. Equally, ways to deal with the likely influx of economic migrants from the former Soviet bloc had to be found. The collapse of communism also created a renewed desire on the part of France to ensure that Germany was locked in to the European integration process (Balme and Woll 2005). During the Cold War, and especially at the start of the EU's history, France was able to dictate terms to a (West) Germany which was seeking to reintegrate itself into the international system. Upon the end of the Cold War, a much wealthier, and much more rehabilitated, Germany might well have been tempted either to dispute French ascendancy within the then-European Community or even to abandon it altogether in favour of a new *Mitteleuropa* which it could lead. Thus, France pushed for deeper European political integration in order to ensure Germany remained a reliable partner in European integration. Other member states either supported this logic or at least accepted that a new system for governing the European continent, with the EU at its core, would have to be developed.

Nonetheless, the negotiations that led to the TEU were far from easy. Maximalists wanted to go for total federation; minimalists wanted to achieve a workable system, but retain control of it at the national level, or at least in the Council, which represents the member states. An emblematically key issue became that of **'subsidiarity'**: the principle of separation of powers between different levels of government. This, of course, is heavily redolent of federalism, which rests on constitutionally-entrenched separation of powers between the various levels and branches of government. However, all that could be agreed was an ambiguous text that stated power should be exercised as closely as possible to the citizen, without stating what that meant, or how it should be decided (Peterson 1994). Other significant and federalism-redolent items included in the TEU were the creation of EU citizenship, which is now enjoyed by all nationals of the member states in addition to their 'domestic' citizenship, the establishment of a clear timetable and set of entry criteria for the single currency, and further institutional change to the benefit of the European Parliament – the 'codecision procedure' (see Chapter 3).

From Maastricht to Lisbon, via the 'Future of Europe'

The Maastricht negotiations, however, marked in a sense the high point of European integration to date. Although subsequent Treaty change at both Amsterdam in 1997 (Devuyst 1998) and Nice in 2000 (Neunreither 2000) saw the introduction of new EU competences, refined decision making procedures, and deepened the integration process, even taken together they represent less of a step forward than the Treaty agreed at Maastricht. The **Nice Treaty** in particular was rather unimpressive – member states descended into the kind of crude power politics that many observers believed had disappeared from EU summits, and managed to make a bitter compromise on the post-'Eastern' enlargement rules for deciding how much each country's vote would count in the Council, and how many seats each member state should have in the European Parliament, but relatively little else. The 2003 failure by the member states to agree a new Treaty after a draft had been created by the Constitutional Convention that they had themselves set up made this trend of diminishing returns even clearer; the eventual rejection of the revised, re-negotiated treaty in 2005, and the lengthy process leading up to the Treaty of Lisbon in 2007, demonstrated further how difficult the process of agreeing new EU Treaties has become.

Indeed, caution about the European integration process may actually have grown at a popular level, resulting in widespread perceptions that the EU suffers from a 'democratic deficit' (Warleigh 2003, Chapters 1 and 2). Thus, although politicians were happy to agree to the Maastricht Treaty, citizens were not always ready to back it in referenda. In France, the referendum was won by the narrowest of majorities; in Denmark, it was lost, and there had to be special negotiations which guaranteed Denmark opt-outs from certain Treaty clauses, and ensured that subsidiarity would in practice be interpreted to defend national sovereignty rather than the powers of the EU itself. Thus, in order to protect the gains that had been made at Maastricht, neither the European Commission nor the member states sought to push further significant new initiatives in the rest of the decade. Instead, efforts were concentrated on securing the launch of the single currency, and on making progress towards enlargement to those countries from the former Soviet bloc which sought it.

The last few years have thus been characterised by occasional events of significance against a backdrop of ongoing, and possibly still incomplete, constitutional reform/Treaty change. In 1999, the European Commission resigned – an unprecedented decision which was taken in order to avoid being sacked by the European Parliament (EP).

BOX 2.4: KEY LEARNING POINT – THE CONTROVERSIAL NATURE OF EUROPEAN INTEGRATION

European integration has always been the subject of fierce debate because it impacts upon a supremely important issue in modern political life: national sovereignty. This controversy has become more widespread in recent years, as the obvious growth of EU power has caused many to worry about its democratic credentials. However, there has always been debate about whether the EU should concentrate on largely economic matters or whether it should embrace a wider range of policies. Here is the heart of the matter: should the EU be 'more than a market'? Opinions about this change over time, and are often different in each member state, at least as regards the degree to which other policies should be adopted, and which ones. It should be remembered, however, that this controversy is not entirely negative. Although public debate on the EU is often conducted in extreme terms and in the absence of facts, the fact that the Union causes such differing reactions is, at least potentially, a means by which greater public engagement with the integration process might be secured because it shows that the EU *matters*.

The relationship between these two institutions has been changing over the last decade, because the balance of power between them has been reversing. At the start of the integration process, the Commission was clearly more important than the Parliament. That is no longer true, and indeed as a legislator it is now the Parliament which has greater influence. Thus, since 1999, the Commission has had to pay greater attention to Parliament and it is no longer quite so clear that, of the **supranational** political institutions it is the Commission which has the greater role (Burns 2002; Cini 2002).

Continuing the recitation of significant events, it must be noted that the single currency, planned since the early days of the EU, was finally launched successfully in 2002. Fifteen member states (initially 12) have now abandoned their national currencies in favour of the euro; three remain outside from choice at the time of writing (Denmark, Sweden and the UK), and the remaining 2004–7 entrants to the Union will have to adopt the euro as soon as they meet the entry criteria, following the lead of Slovenia. The single currency is evidence of the impressive achievements of the EU – no other international organisation in history, as far as we know, has been able to match this accomplishment. The Common Foreign and Security policy also acquired greater momentum when France and the UK – the EU's two leading military states – agreed to co-operate bilaterally. The Union went on to launch a '**Rapid Reaction Force**' (RRF), which, while largely dependent on NATO resources, has given the EU its first troops and distinct military capacity, albeit a small one which is limited to peacekeeping rather than aggressive missions (see Chapter 5).

However, not all the 'events' in European integration would be seen favourably by federalists. Although the Commission's resignation in 1999 was considered testament to the increasing powers of the EP, it also contributed to the EU's public relations problems (Warleigh 2003). Furthermore, the soap opera of Treaty change since the agreement at Nice has been engagingly melodramatic, punctuated by crises over failed referenda and recalcitrant national governments.

After what might diplomatically be described as an awkward summit in Nice, the member states appeared to recognise both that the EU was in need of more widespread change than it had thus far managed, and also that the way in which reform has traditionally been undertaken – an intergovernmental conference leading to a Treaty change at a summit of heads of state/government – had reached the end of its shelf-life. The Nice Treaty, in fact, was rejected by the Irish in a referendum, and although it was subsequently approved by those citizens in a revised form, the idea that a new way of reaching decisions about key issues in the EU gained currency in the national capitals as well as the EU institutions (Lord and Harris 2006: 63–8). The latter had long argued that major reform of the Union should not be a matter for national governments alone.

Thus, the grandly-entitled Convention on the Future of Europe was established by the member states, and tasked with reporting on several key issues of institutional reform, but not policy change, to a further intergovernmental conference, which would in turn produce a new Treaty. The Convention was composed of representatives of the national parliaments and governments of the member states, the European Commission and the European Parliament. It also involved, although without voting rights, representatives of the states which were in the queue to join the EU by 2004. The Convention expanded its remit and set itself the task of producing a draft Constitution for the EU. Initially, there was scepticism that the member states would pay much attention to the Convention, or that they would squeeze out the representatives of both the national parliaments and the EU institutions. In the event, the Convention did produce a Draft Constitution, and, led by senior politicians, appeared to have been taken seriously by the national capitals; nonetheless the member states were unable to agree to adopt the Draft Constitution – or indeed anything else – at the Brussels summit of December 2003.

Under the Irish Presidency of the EU, the member states underwent a high-profile process of negotiation in 2004, trying to agree a revised Constitutional Treaty which would satisfy them all. This was, eventually, duly generated via a diluted version of the Convention-produced draft – only for France and the Netherlands to reject the revised Treaty by popular vote in 2005. In the midst of a major constitutional crisis – deals cut by the member states in the proverbial 'smoke-filled rooms' were no longer considered legitimate as the sole means of shaping new Treaties, and yet the member states could not live with the results of a less intergovernmental means of Treaty change either – the Union launched a 'Year of Reflection', accompanied by various consultation exercises aimed at reaching out to civil society groups as well as national and EU level politicians. This process did at least serve to generate a greater understanding of the real sticking points in securing member state agreement. Eventually, after the German Presidency of 2007 outdid even the Irish Presidency of 2004 for skill in diplomacy and established the basis for a new agreement, the Treaty of Lisbon was signed in December 2007. This Treaty, which was going through the ratification process in the member states as this edition of the book was finalised, retains many elements of the Convention's Draft Constitution, but is watered down by comparison in several respects (see Chapter 6).

CONCEPTUALISING EUROPEAN INTEGRATION: THE IDEA OF 'EUROPEANISATION'

How can this uneven progress and deepening of European integration be conceptualised? The EU represents both a far deeper (i.e. more integrated) and a significantly broader (i.e. encompassing more member states, and enjoying power in more areas of policy) organisation than at its founding, and yet it has not replaced its member states. Indeed, the latter have always been able to prevent further European integration when they so choose (Moravcsik 1999). Moreover, although certain areas of policy have become subject to great influence by the EU, and in a few cases the EU almost entirely controls what happens in member states, other areas have been almost completely kept out of the European integration process – e.g. tax. Furthermore, the acquisition of new powers by the EU has not primarily resulted from either 'spillover' or even the machinations of the Commission – as Monnet would have both hoped and expected – but rather from the deliberate choices of the member states.

A useful way to understand this process – the partial, and willing, transformation by the member states of their own structures and

BOX 2.5: KEY LEARNING POINT – 'EUROPEANISATION'

'Europeanisation' is a helpful concept because it explains the current condition of the integration process in Europe. Instead of seeing the EU as a separate entity from its member states, or as somehow supreme over, or inferior to, them, the Europeanisation idea holds that member states have altered themselves to become part of the EU system. In other words, member states have deliberately allowed their decision-making processes and policies to be altered through a process of **fusion** – both with the EU institutions and with the other member states. This assimilation process is limited, because the powers of the Union are bounded. Thus, member states remain separate entities to a great extent. Nonetheless, they have also entwined themselves together in several important issue areas in order to make sure that they can make effective policy. As a result, there is no separate EU state, and no disappearance of the member states; however, the integration process has come to be a part of the way in which its member states work, and has caused a degree of melding between national and European levels and systems (see Radaelli 2006).

policies by entry into a joint policy-making system – is provided by recent work on the concept of 'Europeanisation'. Although many scholars have used this term to mean different things (see Olsen 2002), the literature on 'Europeanisation' can usefully be understood to refer to three processes:

- the strengthening of central governments in the member states in relation to other domestic actors (such as agencies, interest groups or local/regional government);
- the weakening of central governments, by the ability of other actors such as regional governments or interest groups to by-pass them and create direct relations with EU institutions;
- the transformation of the European state, in which national governments do not wither away but rather work in new patterns of partnership. These partnerships may be short-lived and ill-tempered, but they may also endure. They involve collaborations with EU institutions, other member states, non-governmental actors, and government at local/regional levels. Through this process of transformation, the state is able to maintain its centrality in the system – it changes its *modus operandi*, but as a result it remains powerful (Börzel 2002).

The most useful of the above understandings of 'Europeanisation' is the third, because it is the most broadly encompassing and the most capable of providing an explanation of the mixed, idiosyncratic European Union of today. The idea that European integration has strengthened central governments at the expense of other domestic actors is plausible, but limited: it leaves open questions about why, and to what extent, this has happened. The second understanding appears to be of limited use, because although both regional governments and interest groups of all kinds can indeed work directly with actors at Brussels level, this does not allow them to outflank their central governments on a regular basis on major issues. Because EU decision making requires the creation of coalitions of like-minded actors (see Chapter 3), actors from any member state can secure outcomes that they, rather than their central government, would like if they can generate a sufficient coalition with actors from the EU institutions and other member states (Warleigh 2000). However, outflanking one particular government on one particular issue does not equate to outstripping central government per se. Indeed, given the continued pre-eminence of the Council of Ministers in EU decision-making procedures, actors from outside central governments and whose wishes are opposed by their central governments can only secure the outcomes that they want from EU policy negotiations in partnership with actors from other national governments. Thus, the established wisdom of the 1970s and 1980s – that national governments remain in control of the integration process – is still largely accurate.

However, the third above understanding of 'Europeanisation' can encompass the changes that national governments have experienced in order to retain their centrality. They have undergone a transformation or mutation into central actors in a complex play involving other powerful players from both EU and sub-national (regional/local) levels, as well as non-state actors and those in the wider global system. In this view, EU member states have deliberately transformed themselves as a means of achieving their broader goals – to maintain peace in (Western) Europe, and to ensure the maximum level of economic security. This process has not been easy – the need for it was not always perceived by all the relevant states (e.g. the UK's long sojourn outside the EU) and disagreement about the precise ways in which it should be carried out continues to rage. Nonetheless, the EU's member states have achieved an extraordinary process of transformation, which is set to continue. As a result, 'Europeanisation' is a useful shorthand term to help the reader understand the achievements, limits and complexities of the European integration process to date.

THINK POINTS

- Why didn't the member states of the EU simply create a United States of Europe after the Second World War?
- Why has the evolution of European integration been uneven?
- What role has European law played in the evolution of European integration?
- Why has economic integration been easier to achieve than political integration?
- Why has the process of Treaty change become more complex, as well as more controversial, since 2000?

FURTHER READING

Cini, Michelle (ed.) (2006) *European Union Politics* (2nd edn) (Oxford: Oxford University Press).
An excellent and accessible textbook on the history, policies and controversies of the European Union.

Dinan, Desmond (2004) *Europe Recast: A History of European Union* (Basingstoke: Palgrave).
An accessible introductory history of the EU.

Magnette, Paul (2005) *What is the European Union? Nature and Prospects* (Basingstoke: Palgrave).
A first-rate analysis of the EU and how its character affects its evolution.

INSTITUTIONS AND DECISION-MAKING IN THE EUROPEAN UNION

The manner in which the European Union (EU) produces public policy is complex. Given that the needs and interests of the various member governments must be taken into account in order to reach a compromise that they can all accept, this is not surprising. Furthermore, parties other than national governments play a role in the process. The EU's own institutions have a significant amount of power, and it is clear that these institutions often seek to follow their own priorities rather than those of the member states. Individuals and groups from civil society, and private interest groups (bodies which represent trades, manufacturers and professions) are also often able to influence decisions made in Brussels and Strasbourg, the seats of the EU's main political institutions.

Thus, the aim of this chapter is to focus on three principal issues. First, I explain the structure of the EU's decision-making system. Second, I introduce the EU institutions with the greatest impact on public policy making at the Union level. Third, I discuss the operations of the EU system. The third section is perhaps the most important, because although it is vital to comprehend the structures and institutions of the Union, such knowledge is far more useful when it is wedded to an understanding of how the EU actually works.

I: THE STRUCTURE OF THE EUROPEAN UNION

As has been pointed out already, the EU has a novel structure. This structure helps us to understand the ways in which the Union is both a political system with extensive powers in its own right and yet also extremely dependent upon its member states. This is because the EU structure reveals that although European integration can encompass many different policy issues, it has not made the member states redundant as the key deciders of policy, although it *has* made them both more interdependent, and rather less autonomous.

The Maastricht Treaty created the 'European Union' by adding further competences to those that the previous incarnation of the integration process, the European Community, enjoyed. To some extent, this was an exercise in re-branding: as part of the move to promote the idea that European integration had deepened considerably, the name 'Union' was substituted for 'Community'. However, there are also matters of substance to be observed in the change of name. This is for two reasons. First, the fact that the integration process *was* deepened by Maastricht – it brought about many innovations, such as further powers for the EP, the detailed time-line and plans for the adoption of the euro, and EU citizenship. Second, the

---

BOX 3.1: KEY LEARNING POINT – THE THREE PILLARS OF THE EU, AS BEFORE THE TREATY OF LISBON

PILLAR	TITLE	KEY FUNCTIONS	SUPRA-NATIONAL?
I	European Community	Single market and 'flanking policies'	Yes
II	Common Foreign and Security Policy	Foreign and defence policies	No
III	Police and Judicial Co-operation in Criminal Matters	Cross-border crime; anti-terrorism policy	No

fact that although this deepening of the integration process was real, it was also limited. The Maastricht Treaty gave what we know as the EU the beginnings of competence in major new areas: foreign/defence policy, the fight against crime, and immigration policy. But it did not create a federal United States of Europe, as certain member governments had wished.

In order to achieve the step from Community to Union, the member states compromised between those which wanted to go further, and those which had strong reservations. The Union system was created, but it was split into three so-called pillars. The first pillar, the European Community, was by far the most important in terms of volume of legislation, and it essentially comprised all the areas of competence that the member states had previously agreed to pool at the European level. Pillar II comprised the Common Foreign and Security Policy, an ambitious project which is still in its infancy – although the beginnings of an EU role in military affairs can be seen from its leadership of peace-keeping missions in areas such as the Congo. Pillar III was entitled 'Justice and Home Affairs', although it was re-named 'Police and Judicial Cooperation in Criminal Matters' by the subsequent **Amsterdam Treaty** (1997). Like Pillar II, the potential for progress in this pillar was thus placed under clear initial limits. In recent years, however, there has been a significant increase in attempts to foster European-level co-operation in migration and asylum policies, as well as the fight against drugs, organised crime and terrorism. Indeed, in line with plans introduced in the Amsterdam Treaty, many aspects of these policy areas have been switched to Pillar I (Uçarer 2006: 309–11).

There are two keys to understanding the Union's split structure. The first is appreciating the difference in the respective decision rules of each pillar, i.e. how policy is made in each of them. Pillar I is supranational – in other words, the EU's institutions have their full range of powers, and the member states are no longer independent. Pillars II and III, however, are intergovernmental. In other words, in these pillars only the Council – and thus the member states – has power. Thus, the 'European Union' is a term which properly refers to the three pillars as a collective organisation, i.e. European Community + Common Foreign and Security Policy + Police and Judicial Co-operation in Criminal Matters. Strictly speaking, matters of the first pillar remain 'European Community' issues. Hence, the correct term is 'EC law' rather than 'EU law'; the Commission's full name remains the Commission of the European Communities, rather than Commission of the European Union. This terminology matters because it means that the scope of EC law is limited. It also demonstrates that on the issues which they consider most sensitive, the member states can retain power for themselves and rule out intervention by the Commission, Court and Parliament. This should be borne in mind, although throughout this book, as in most academic and media coverage, the term 'EU' is often used whatever the 'pillar' for the sake of convenience.

The second key, however, requires an understanding that the pillar structure is flexible rather than fixed. The arrangements made at Maastricht were modified at Amsterdam, particularly regarding the 'communitarisation' of many third pillar issues, i.e. their re-location into Pillar I. If it is ratified, the Treaty of Lisbon will make further changes to this structure (see Chapter 6). Thus, the calculations

BOX 3.2: KEY LEARNING POINT– THE FIVE MAIN INSTITUTIONS OF THE EU

INSTITUTION	MAIN SEAT	MAIN FUNCTION
Council of the European Union ('Council of Ministers')	Brussels	Legislation and setting the EU budget
Commission	Brussels	Proposing legislation; overseeing the running of the EU system; external representation of the EU
European Parliament	Brussels and Strasbourg	Legislation and setting the EU budget
European Central Bank	Frankfurt	Managing the single currency
European Court of Justice	Luxembourg	Ensuring that EC law is upheld

and agreements between the member states about how sensitive issues such as immigration are addressed at EU level are capable of deeper Europeanisation after the initial moment of introducing EU competence.

II: PRINCIPAL INSTITUTIONS OF THE EUROPEAN UNION[1]

The Council of the European Union

The Council of the European Union, otherwise known as the Council of Ministers or simply 'the Council', is the most powerful of all the EU institutions in terms of day-to-day politics.[2] It represents the member governments, and no EU legislation is possible without the Council's agreement. It is the ultimate and main legislator of the EU. The Council is also, together with the European Parliament (EP), the EU's budgetary authority.

The membership of the Council changes according to the issue at hand, but it always consists of ministers from the member governments.[3] Thus, if the issue is fixing subsidies to farmers, the Council will consist of national agriculture ministers and will be known as the 'Agriculture Council'; if the issue is the struggle against air pollution, the Council will consist of national environment ministers and be known as the 'Environment Council', and so on. The General Affairs Council is the most important of the Council's incarnations. It consists of the foreign ministers of the member states, and has a remit which is much broader than those of the 'sectoral' Councils such as those mentioned immediately above.

The Council is led by a President, with each member state in turn holding the Council Presidency for six months. Each member state has an allocation of votes in the Council, which are 'weighted' in order roughly to reflect that state's population size. Thus, Germany has more votes in the Council than Ireland or Latvia. The Council usually makes decisions by generating a consensus between its members. Until the Single European Act (SEA), indeed, this was the only way in which it could work, because the Treaty obliged the member states to agree legislation unanimously. After the SEA, however, the Council has been able in many cases to work on the basis of qualified majority voting (QMV). This change in the way the Council worked was introduced in order to ensure that on certain key policy issues no single member state could prevent the Union as a whole from making policy. In practice, however, very few matters are actually put to the vote in the Council, since the member states generally prefer to accommodate each other's preferences in order to ensure that their own preferences will be taken into account subsequently (Sherrington 2000).

The Council's work is prepared by the various national civil services (working for their own ministers) as well as several preparatory bodies at the EU level. Of these, two are the most important. The first is the Committee of Permanent Representatives, known as 'Coreper' after its French acronym. This brings together high-level diplomats – ambassadors to the EU in all but name – from each member state in order to negotiate and resolve as many problems as possible, in order to leave only the most troublesome issues to the Council itself. The second is the Council Secretariat, which functions as the institution's own bureaucracy.

The Commission of the European Communities

The Commission of the European Communities (the European Commission, the Commission) is a unique institution which is both a kind of civil service for the EU and a political animal in its own right. The Commission's main duties are to initiate proposals for EU legislation, to act as EU-level regulator, that is, to be the so-called 'Guardian of the Treaties', with a duty to ensure that the member states abide by the commitments they have made in EU politics, and to act as the EU's external representative, particularly on matters of trade relations with the rest of the world. The Commission has also often been seen as the body which represents the general EU interest, rather than those of any particular member state. For this reason, the Commission is regularly considered to be an ally by the 'small' member states (those with small populations and thus fewer votes in the Council).

The Commission has also been seen as a government-in-waiting: one of the Commission's key functions according to the original design of the EU was to shepherd the integration process forward until a European Federation was created and the Commission could become its government. Instead, the role of the Commission has been limited, first by the creation of the European Council as the strategic agenda-setter for the Union (Bulmer 1996), and subsequently since the 1990s brought both increases in power for the EP (see below) and the scandals over financial mismanagement and inappropriate working practices which caused the resignation of the entire College of Commissioners in 1999. Although the Commission still has a political role – notably in terms of external economic policy and through its ability to accept or reject amendments to its proposals for legislation by the EP – it is nowadays rather less central to the EU's policy-making process than in the early days of European integration.

The Commission has a President, who is nominated by the Council, but who must receive the approval of a majority of members in the EP before he or she can take office. The Commission also has a College, a kind of executive body, which consists of one Commissioner from each member state. Within the College, certain portfolios are often considered to be more prestigious than others, usually because they correspond to an issue area in which the Commission has significant powers – such as external trade. The Commissioners are chosen by the Commission President from a list of nominees supplied by the member states. Nominated Commissioners attend a hearing in the EP, which must confirm their collective nomination as the new College. In 2004, the EP objected to two of the nominated Commissioners, and as a result refused to approve the new College. Replacement nominations were made before the EP gave its approval – a further indication that the Commission is increasingly accountable to the EP.

As of January 2008, there are 27 Commissioners, including the President (José Manuel Barroso) and five Vice-Presidents. The Commission is responsible for 40 Directorates General (DGs), each of which is effectively a civil service department responsible for a particular issue area in which the EU has competence, with each DG ultimately accountable to a particular Commissioner. The vast majority of Commission staff are not politicians but rather bureaucrats, i.e. they are civil servants.

The European Parliament

The European Parliament (the EP) is the EU's only directly elected institution. It consists of members (MEPs) elected in each member state, who sit in cross-national party groups or as independents rather than as members of national delegations. MEPs have five-year renewable terms of office, and each member state sends an allotted number of MEPs, again according to a formula which roughly reflects the population size of each member state. Thus, the UK has more MEPs than Denmark, and Poland has more than Estonia. The EP has become far more important over the course of European integration. Initially, it was usually considered to be a powerless 'talking shop' on the fringes of EU decision-making. Over time, however, as a result of various Treaty changes since the SEA, the EP has become a powerful part of the EU legislative system, particularly when the co-decision procedure applies (see Section III). It is also, together with the Council, the body which agrees the EU budget. The EP also acts as supervisor of the Commission, particularly with regard to how the Commission has spent the EU budget. It appoints certain key office-holders in the EU, such as the President and College of the Commission, or the Ombudsman, who investigates allegations of maladministration against the EU bodies.[4] Finally, the EP can dismiss the entire College of Commissioners for malpractice – the power known as the right of censure.

The EP works primarily through its various committees, all of which include MEPs from the different party groups and member states. EP committees focus on a particular issue area – for example social policy, or fisheries policy. As the Treaty gives the EP more power in certain policy areas than in others, there is an informal hierarchy of committees in the EP, which often makes membership of those committees that correspond to the areas in which the EP has been given greatest powers highly sought-after. For example, membership of the Committee on the Environment, Public Health and Food Safety might be seen as more advantageous or prestigious than membership of the Committee on Petitions. Plenary sessions, in which the MEPs formally vote on the EP's position on policy issues, occur in Brussels and Strasbourg. Most of the EP's work, however, is done in Brussels; the monthly trek to Strasbourg, a relic from the Parliament's powerless past, is continued against the EP's will at the insistence of the French government.

The **European Central Bank** (ECB) is a recently-established EU institution. It came into being in 1998 as part of the preparations for the launch of the European single currency, the euro, which was itself launched 'virtually' in 1999. The physical entry into circulation of euro notes and coins took place in 2002. The ECB is an unusual EU institution in two ways. First, it is completely independent of the more overtly political institutions (Council, Commission, Parliament). This is to ensure that EU monetary policy is seen to be free from political manoeuvring. Second, it is based not in Brussels, but in Frankfurt. The ECB has a narrow, but vital, task: to ensure the single currency functions well. The Treaty gives it one principal method of meeting this duty – to ensure that inflation remains very low in the euro-zone, i.e. the countries which have adopted the euro. At the time of writing, this involves Germany, Spain, Italy, Slovenia, France, Portugal, Malta, Greece, the Netherlands, Belgium, Cyprus, Luxembourg, Austria, Finland and Ireland.

The ECB has an Executive Board and a Governing Council. The Executive Board comprises the President, Vice-President and four independent experts, all of whom are appointed by the Council of Ministers for non-renewable terms of eight years. The Governing Council consists of the members of the Executive Board, plus the governors of the central banks of each participating member state. All voting is by simple majority, with each member having one vote – there are no 'weighted votes' in the ECB. However, in the early years of the ECB, the tendency has been to seek consensus rather than put matters to vote (Howarth 2002).

The ECB also co-operates with the central banks of those countries which are member states of the EU, but which have not adopted the euro – either because they do not wish to, or because they do not yet meet the criteria for membership. This co-operation takes place within the European System of Central Banks (ESCB), which brings together the governors of the central banks of each member state of the EU. Those from outside the euro-zone have no right to vote on matters of single currency monetary policy. However, the ESCB is a useful forum to address issues which affect all member states of the EU, whether they have adopted the euro or not.

The European Court of Justice

The European Court of Justice (ECJ, the Court) is the final major institution of the EU. It has no direct role to play in the process of making EU policy, but its powers to interpret the Treaties have allowed it to make decisions which have, in some cases, had a major impact on the way the EU as a whole has developed. The ECJ sits in Luxembourg, and consists of one judge per member state, along with eight Advocates General, whose task is to present independent opinions on all cases brought before the Court. Although each member state appoints a member to the Court, every member of the ECJ is expected to be neutral in her or his views. They are expected to bring experience of their respective legal systems, but not formally to represent their national government. The Court can sit either in full, in Grand Chamber of 13 Justices, or in small Chambers of three or five Justices, according to the provisions of its Statute and requests from a party to a dispute.

The ECJ hears cases which concern either *adjudication* or *interpretation*. The Court's adjudication role requires it to judge whether particular acts or proposals are illegal, because they overstep the limits of power granted by the Treaties, or whether member states are at fault for incorrect or incomplete implementation of agreed policy. The Court's interpretation function requires it to rule on the precise meaning of the Treaties, assisting the courts of the member states in the correct application of EC law. The ECJ has been assisted by a **Court of First Instance** (CFI) since 1998. The CFI is perhaps best considered as a junior chamber of the ECJ; it reduces the volume of cases that the ECJ must hear, and specialises in actions brought by private actors such as individuals or companies against acts of the EU institutions. Like the ECJ, the CFI has one justice from each member state, but it has no Advocates General.

Other institutions and bodies of the EU include the **Court of Auditors**, the **Ombudsman**, the **Economic and Social Committee** (EESC) and the **Committee of the Regions** (CoR). The role played by these bodies in the policy-making process is generally small, either because they are concerned in specialist ways with overseeing the way the principal political institutions work (Court of Auditors, Ombudsman), or because they have weak legislative powers (EESC, CoR).

The Court of Auditors acts as the EU's independent financial watchdog. It reports on the propriety of how the EU runs its finances, and can be extremely influential given the importance of honest financial management. It was the Court of Auditors' report on the 1996 budget, which was highly critical, that sparked the chain of events leading to the resignation of the Commission in 1999.

The position of EU Ombudsman was established in the Maastricht Treaty. The Ombudsman is appointed by the EP, and is tasked with ensuring that the EU is properly administered. The Ombudsman can respond to complaints from citizens, or investigate issues under his/her own initiative. In its short history to date, the office of Ombudsman has had an impact on the policy-making process by promoting further transparency and defending citizens' interests. However, because the Ombudsman has no power to impose a settlement on an erring institution, but must rather *negotiate* a settlement, the impact of the office has so far been less extensive than it might otherwise be. Its impact has also been reduced by the fact that it cannot pursue allegations of malpractice against the member governments, even when they act as implementers of EU policy. Instead, the Ombudsman's remit refers only to the EU's other institutions.

The EESC and CoR are advisory committees, created to give specialist advice to the policy-making institutions (Council, EP, Commission) on legislative proposals. The EESC was established at the outset of European integration and brings together the 'social partners' (employers and trades unions) plus other representatives of civil society; the CoR was set up by the Maastricht Treaty, and brings together representatives of regional and local governments from the member states. Although both these bodies can have an impact on policy made at the EU level, this is not usually extensive. The EESC has tended to be overlooked by interest groups, which prefer to lobby EU institutions directly and on their own initiative, rather than be constrained by the need to reach agreement with other interest groups in order to produce a coherent EESC position. The CoR has not yet completely established itself as a powerful voice for subnational authorities, chiefly because many of its most important members (in terms of their domestic powers) prefer to use other means of influence, usually direct lobbying or collaboration with their respective national governments.

III: DECISION-MAKING IN THE EU: THE IMPORTANCE OF ALLIANCE-BUILDING

Understanding decision-making in the EU requires some effort. This is because the process through which it happens is complex. It is also because, as stated above, each of the Pillars functions differently, with power much more clearly reserved for the member states in the Council in Pillars II and III than in Pillar I. This pillar produces the bulk of EU policy by a complex process which involves

BOX 3.3: KEY LEARNING POINT – TYPES OF
          DECISION IN THE EU

TYPE OF DECISION	DEGREE OF 'BINDINGNESS'
Decision	Completely binding on a specific actor, or group, but not capable of being generally applied.
Regulation	Completely and generally binding, both regarding the substance of policy and the manner in which it must be implemented.
Directive	Binding regarding the policy outcome, but free regarding the manner in which the policy is implemented.

people – 'actors' – from each of the EU institutions, national governments, civil society, and sometimes regional or local government in a
struggle to make alliances with sufficient numbers of others in order
to carry the day when the proposal comes to vote. Moreover, there
are different types of decision that can be made, and three principal
procedures through which they arise.

The types of decision are *regulations*, *directives* and *decisions*. These
differ in the degree to which they are binding on the member states or
the specific legal persons to which they are applied (see Box 3.3).

The great bulk of EU policy is in the form of 'directives', which
gives the member states the maximum leeway on issues of implementation. This is important because it allows the different national
systems to find their own methods of achieving an agreed common
goal. It also means, however, that the EU institutions have fewer
powers to oversee implementation of policy than might otherwise be
the case.

The three legislative processes are *consultation*, *assent* and
co-decision (see Box 3.4).

These differ in the degree of power that is given to the EP. The
Treaty states which type of decision, and which process, is appropriate in each case.

BOX 3.4: KEY LEARNING POINT –
EU DECISION-MAKING PROCESSES

LEGISLATIVE PROCESS	POWERS OF THE EUROPEAN PARLIAMENT
Consultation	EP must be asked for its opinion, but has no means to oblige the Council to accept it.
Assent	EP has the power to veto, but not amend, legislation.
Co-decision	EP has the power to amend, and ultimately veto, legislation.

As a mark of the rise of the EP in terms of its legislative role, it should be noted that the great majority of legislative proposals are now subject to the co-decision procedure, which gives a roughly equal say over policy-making to the Parliament and the Council. Indeed, co-decision is now often referred to as the 'normal' or 'ordinary' legislative procedure – a far cry from the early days of European integration. The consultation procedure, by contrast, is a throw-back to the 1950s, and is used in a decreasing number of areas. The assent procedure was established in the SEA, and applies to a small number of issues, including certain important questions, such as accession treaties for new member states. Thus, in principle, the EP could bar a candidate country from joining the EU.

A further complicating feature of the EU policy-making system is the fact that there is no clear separation of powers either vertically, i.e. between the EU and the member states, or horizontally, i.e. between the EU institutions.

As part of the process of Europeanisation discussed in Chapter 2, EU practice has been to blur the distinction between EU and national levels of decision-making to a significant extent. The principle of subsidiarity is supposed to clarify this situation, but has not yet done so because the EU is still evolving. It is not yet possible to state which areas of policy must remain definitively outside the scope of the EU – not least because the various member states all have different views on that subject, and these views can change over time.

Furthermore, the point at which the powers of each EU institution can be said to end is also best described as fuzzy – at least as far as the Council, Commission and Parliament are concerned. This is because the classic functions of government are deliberately blurred in the EU. There is, clearly, a separate judiciary – the ECJ and CFI, in conjunction with the national legal systems. But the executive and legislative functions of the EU are mixed responsibilities. The task of being the EU's executive – that is, holding the responsibility for ensuring that EU policy is carried out properly – is chiefly performed by the Commission, with the ECJ also given powers to rule in cases of alleged non-compliance with EU policy by member states. However, given the trend towards new modes of policy-making, such as bench-marking and best practice exchange, which allow the member states to co-ordinate their policies without creating a new common European policy (see Chapter 4), it is arguable that the member states are also given an executive role insofar as they are in some way made responsible for their own compliance with the measures they have agreed.

The legislative function of the EU is a triangle between the Council, Parliament and Commission. Formally speaking in Pillar I, no legislative proposal can be made unless it comes from the Commission, which gives the latter significant power over the EU agenda, although both the Council and the EP have been known to make successful requests for a proposal to the Commission. Moreover, even under the co-decision procedure, the Commission plays a key role in the early stages of the decision-making process, and is able to shape the positions adopted by the EP and Council. At the other end of the process, formal decisions about the content of policy are left to the Council and EP – under assent and co-decision, both institutions must agree the content of policy for it to reach the statute book.

A useful way to think about the EU policy process is through the metaphor of the policy chain. This helps the observer remember that the policy-making process is an interlocking one, and that what happens at one stage of the process has an impact on what happens at the next stage, either by opening up new possibilities or by restricting the scope for action. Indeed, the real-world process of decision-making often shows that it is hard to place the boundaries between stages in the decision-making process. With that caveat in mind, schematically a typical policy chain for a hypothetical directive proposed using the co-decision process might look as in Box 3.5.

BOX 3.5: KEY LEARNING POINT – POLICY CHAIN FOR A HYPOTHETICAL DIRECTIVE

POLICY STAGE	ACTIVITY
Proposal planning	Commission drafts proposal, after consultation with outside interest groups, MEPs and national governments.
Proposal issuing	Commission publishes proposal, normally after internal debate between different Directorates General.
Scrutiny	Proposal is scrutinised by the national governments, EP, interest groups and advisory committees (EESC, CoR).
Consensus formation	Member states attempt to reach a Common Position in Council; EP generates a consensus in committee and then secures plenary support. Interest groups and advisory committees produce analysis papers and suggestions for amendments.
Amendment	Council, EP return their respective amended drafts, which often reflect the desires of interest groups, to the Commission.
Re-issue	Commission re-issues a revised proposal.
Second scrutiny	Council, EP decide their respective positions on the revised draft.
Legislation	Council and EP agree text of new law, either immediately or after convening a 'conciliation committee' to resolve their differences.
Implementation	New directive becomes law in each member state. Its implementation is monitored by interest groups.
Adjudication (if necessary)	Implementation is found to be insufficient – interest group reports the member state in question to the Commission, which can prosecute the state in question at the ECJ.

Unsurprisingly, given the labyrinthine qualities of the decision-making process, it is common for actors to seek to further their causes by lobbying others who will have a say in the content of the legislation. This process of *hustling* (Warleigh 2000) begins before the proposal is published, as those with an interest in the subject of the proposed legislation attempt to shape its content right from the outset. The Commission is also often open to input from member states and the EP, because it has an interest in ensuring that as much of the proposal as possible makes it onto the statute book. Thus, there is absolutely no point in attempting to include something which it is clear either a majority of either member states or MEPs will not support. The Commission must also secure the support of all its internal stakeholders – that is, it must generate agreement between all its Directorates General (DGs) about what should be included in the proposal. This can be a difficult process, as different DGs may have widely differing views on the subject – for example, the priorities of DG Enterprise and Industry may well be out of sympathy with those of DG Environment.

Once the proposal is public, the hustling becomes even more intensive. Further interest groups will mobilise – initial consultations inside the Commission tend to involve fewer groups than those outside. Public positions are taken by MEPs and Council members. They also receive input from the EESC and CoR. Institutional positions begin to emerge in both the Council and the EP. Intriguingly, however, behind the scenes there is often regular contact between national ministers, Coreper and MEPs at this stage, in order to prepare the ground for a possible conciliation process, or even avoid it altogether. Co-decision requires a qualified majority in the Council and an absolute majority of MEPs to support the proposal. Thus, it is quite logical for those with a stake in the outcome to make alliances with other actors who hold similar views in the other institution, not simply their own: an MEP with a keen interest in preventing air pollution, for example, would be far more likely to impact on the content of the directive by persuading a majority of her colleagues and member states with the required votes in the Council than by getting unanimous support in the EP and only 50% of the votes in the other institution. As a result, complex coalitions involving actors from EU institutions, national governments and interest groups are formed.

Both the Council and the EP send their amended versions of the proposal back to the Commission. The Commission then seeks to produce a revised draft which will satisfy both the other institutions. If this is impossible, the remaining points of dispute are clarified, and a 'conciliation committee' is convened. This committee involves equal numbers of representatives from the EP and the Council. Its task is to broker inter-institutional agreement on outstanding problems with the proposed directive. If the conciliation committee is unsuccessful, the legislation falls. If it works out, the legislation is passed, providing that the relevant majorities in the Council and the EP are assembled; if they are not, then the legislation falls. In practice, conciliation committees almost always produce agreement, and the Council and the Parliament often agree an outcome before it is necessary to invoke the conciliation process.

Once the legislation is on the statute book, it is up to the member states to implement it. This they do according to their own constitutions: some may give the responsibility to national ministries, others to regional governments, others to specialist agencies, etc. However this is done, the end outcome must be the same: the agreed standards must be met. If they are not, the member state in question can be taken to the ECJ, and prosecuted. However, this is not an easy process: the Commission has no powers to inspect policy implementation, except in competition and agriculture policies, so it is reliant upon members of the public or interest groups to report problems to it. Once allegations are made, the Commission must decide whether or not to take the case to the ECJ: it may refuse to do so, either because the evidence is not sufficient, or because it considers that a direct challenge to the particular member state would be unwise in the prevailing circumstances. However, such cases do occur, and the right of the Court to impose fines for non-compliance was written into the Treaty at Maastricht.

Thus, the policy chain of the EU is complex, but suitable for producing workable policy. Despite its intricacy, it is able to involve a great array of actors, and it has proven to be capable of both evolution over time and application to growing numbers of issue areas. In the next chapter, I examine the output of this system in terms of some of its key policies.

THINK POINTS

- What does the changing pillar structure indicate about the balance between national sovereignty and European-level federalism in the Union?

- What do the rise of the EP and relative decline of the Commission imply about the member states' plans for the EU?
- What does the reliance upon directives rather than regulations as forms of legislation tell us about the nature of the Union?
- Why is it so necessary to 'hustle' in order to make policy in the EU system? Would it be better, or worse, to have a clearer separation of powers between the EU institutions, and between the Union and the member states?

FURTHER READING

Hix, Simon (2005) *The Political System of the European Union* (2nd edn) (London: Palgrave).
The first book-length treatment of the contemporary Union as a policy-making system in its own right: an extremely useful book, now in a second edition.

Peterson, John and Shackleton, Michael (eds) (2006) *The Institutions of the European Union* (2nd edn) (Oxford: Oxford University Press).
A thorough and informative guide to the EU's institutions and bodies.

Phinnemore, David and Warleigh-Lack, Alex (eds) (2008) *Reflections on European Integration* (Basingstoke: Palgrave).
A wide-ranging set of essays by both leading academics and EU policy-makers, reflecting on the developments in both the EU and in EU studies over the last 50 years.

Richardson, Jeremy (ed.) (2006) *European Union Power and Policy-Making* (2nd edn) (London: Routledge).
A collection of excellent essays on the Union's institutions, policy-making system, and main functions.

Warleigh, Alex (ed.) (2002) *Understanding European Union Institutions* (London: Routledge).
A useful and easy to read set of essays on each of the EU institutions and bodies.

KEY POLICIES OF THE EUROPEAN UNION

I: INTRODUCTION

In this chapter I discuss the range of European Union's (EU's) internal policies, i.e. those which apply chiefly to its member states rather than the rest of the world. Although it is not always possible clearly to separate the internal from the external in terms of the nature of a public policy – as the very existence of the EU makes clear – this is a conventional way of categorising policy competences heuristically. I adopt the categorisation here, but the reader should bear in mind that the distinction between internal and external is at best fuzzy: to give two examples which are explored in more detail below, the single market was established for reasons of both internal and external policy, and the EU's environment policy has been developed with a similarly complex rationale.

In order to discuss EU internal policies, I set out the principal areas in which the EU has the power to act and explain why it has certain competences but not others. I also discuss the issue of what I call policy style: the approach to policy-making taken by the EU. This has links with the discussion of decision-making presented in Chapter 3. However, it is not the same subject. *Policy-making procedures* are structural, that is, they are established by rules of the Treaty, relating to and even helping to create the political system of the EU itself.

Policy styles, on the other hand, are the ways in which EU actors use the procedures, or even go outside them, to make policy. This chiefly relates to whether traditional, or 'hard' policy is preferred to more recent forms of 'soft policy' such as the Open Method of Coordination (OMC), which tend to emphasise guidance and standards to be achieved instead of imposing a detailed requirement to legislate. Finally, I outline the main policies of the EU.

II: THE EU'S POLICY RANGE: WHAT THE UNION CAN DO, AND WHAT IT CANNOT

The areas in which the EU can make policy continue to change over time. The general trend has been for a significant growth: with co-operation beginning in areas of steel and coal production, the EU has in the nearly 60 years from Paris to Lisbon reached the point at which it is legally competent to make policy in many diverse areas such as foreign affairs, agriculture and consumer protection.

However, key areas of policy remain outside its official competence. It is true that the EU has always had the ability to use a provision in the Treaty to make decisions in an area in which it had not been given competence, if this is necessary to achieve a goal with which it has been tasked. In practice, though, this article has been used relatively infrequently, because the EU would otherwise have come under severe attack from the member states. National governments have in general preferred either to give the EU new competences by means of Treaty reform where necessary, or to do without EU activity in a given area of policy. This is certainly true in matters of primary legislation, i.e. the Treaties themselves, which set out whether the EU has exclusive, shared, or no competence in a policy area (see Box 4.1). In matters of secondary legislation – i.e. the policies made by the EU in order to meet the responsibilities given to it by the Treaties – there has been considerably more scope to develop legislation without the specific permission of the Treaty. Perhaps the most famous example is environment policy: before the Single European Act (SEA), the EU had no official competence in environmental protection, but nonetheless many directives and regulations with environmental implications had been made as part of the drive for common policy in other areas.

The EU's main internal policy areas can be classified as: market-making measures; and market-support measures.

BOX 4.1: KEY LEARNING POINT – COMPETENCES
OF THE EU

The EU has different kinds of competence, on a spectrum from 'exclusive competence', i.e. areas where the member states have formally agreed to abandon their powers to the Union, to 'member state competence', that is, areas which have been specifically placed outside the EU remit by Treaty. 'Concurrent competence' is close to the 'exclusive' end of the spectrum: it refers to areas in which the member states can make policy individually until such time as the EU legislates in that area, at which point it becomes an EU competence. The key issue here is thus at what point, if ever, the EU proposes legislation. Finally, 'complementary competence' is closer to the 'member state competence' end of the spectrum. It gives the EU power to legislate in order to support national legislation, but not to replace it.

Market-making measures

The EU's principal competences are in the field of economic and trade policy. The original goal of the EU, after all, was to build such intricate economic ties between its member states that war between them would become unthinkable. Over time, this competence has been symbolised by three hugely important initiatives: competition policy (which seeks to ensure fair competition across the EU for companies and other economic actors from each member state), the single market, and the single currency. The EU's powers in competition policy are extensive: EU inspectors can and do ensure that no unfair barriers are placed in the way of businesses seeking to break out of their national markets and enter those of other member states. As such, it is the keystone of the single market initiative (whose objective was to promote and facilitate economic growth), which is in turn vital to the success of the euro. In these areas of policy, member states have ceded almost all power to the EU.

Market support measures

The EU also has powers in areas which have been considered vital to the creation of the single European market (SEM), either to help its creation or to lessen its negative impact on particular social groups and geographical areas.

The first example of such activity can be found in the EU's Common Agricultural Policy (CAP), which was designed to ensure that the member states would have a sufficient food supply to re-build after the devastation of the Second World War. As a result, the EU's role in providing subsidies to farmers and protecting EU agriculture from overseas competition has been of great importance. Historically, this policy has also taken up the great majority of the EU's budget, although in recent years the trend has been to reduce the amount spent on agriculture and increase the amount spent on regional policy. This policy – regional/cohesion policy – is another unique feature of the Union. In no other international organisation do member states provide financial compensation to others which are unable to benefit so readily from common policies, either because they are geographically peripheral or because they are suffering from a particular economic hardship such as the decline of heavy industry. Taken together with social policy – an area in which the EU has limited, but growing competence – this gives the EU impressive responsibilities in redistributive politics (or solidarity between the different member states and their regions), which have no, or weak, echoes in other international organisations.

Further EU activities which can be treated as market-support measures are environmental, public health and consumer protection policies. This is not to say that protecting the EU market is always the primary goal of EU action in this area. However, the primary justification for EU activity in such 'flanking measures' has always been the argument that it is necessary for the optimal benefit of the single market to be realised. Such was the argument made by Jacques Delors, for example, when as Commission President he sought to deepen EU activity in the social arena by linking it to the need to ensure that the single market made nobody worse off than they would otherwise have been. Thus, as the single market has reached nearer and nearer to completion, EU-level co-operation in areas such as consumer protection and environmental policy has often increased, in order to ensure that neither consumers nor the environment suffer unduly from the consequences of economic integration either through the loss of rights or through the promotion of lowest common denominator, rather than more environmentally friendly, policy.

This list of powers is impressive. No international organisation can match the EU for range and depth of policy competence. However, it is worth recalling that the EU is unable to act in many key areas of policy. For its part, the EU is not, at least for the present, able to match the range of competences enjoyed by its member states despite the fact that it is the world's most powerful international organisation. Vital matters of policy in which the EU has no or very limited power to act include: *taxation* and *fiscal policy* (the single currency gives the EU authority in monetary policy only); *defence* (there is no standing EU army; instead, the EU is beginning to use its **Rapid Reaction Force**, composed of troops from member state armies, within the auspices of NATO, for humanitarian or peace-keeping measures); and *the budget* (the member states agree how much of their **GDP** they will give to the EU – currently, this figure is just over 1%; the EU has no power to raise its own revenue through tax).

III: EXPLAINING THE IMPRESSIVE-BUT-LIMITED POLICY COMPETENCE OF THE EU

There are many factors which explain the limitations of EU competence to date. Perhaps the best place to look for the beginnings of an explanation is in the European policies of the USA. At the time of the EU's inception, the role of the USA in both promoting European integration and limiting the development of the EU was crucial. The USA wanted to ensure that Europe was economically regenerated, and thus able to serve as a trading partner for the USA; it also wanted to ensure that Western Europe remained outside the communist bloc. Economic integration of as much of Europe as possible suited the USA admirably. What the USA did not want was to see the emergence of a rival. Thus, West European defence was provided by an organisation in which the USA played, and still plays, the key role (namely NATO). Moreover, the Cold War insecurity increased the dependence of the EU states on the protection of the USA. The military might of the latter, when lent to the EU states via NATO, provided a disincentive for the EU to develop its own defence capacities, even had the economic capacity and political will to take such a step been present. Why should Europeans pay for their common defence when the USA was ready to foot the bill in the name of the fight against communism (Lundestad 1986)?

A related issue is that of national sovereignty. Given their ability to rely on the USA for many of their defence policy needs, the member states were able to adopt a more rigorous approach to their respective autonomies when dealing with each other than might otherwise have been the case. They did not have to form a federation, seeking a common defence policy in order to withstand potential enemies elsewhere. Thus, the member states' approach to European integration has tended to be utilitarian rather than idealistic: national sovereignty has been shared at the EU level when the member states can agree that this would be likely to bring significant benefits, and preserved as far as possible when such gains were not considered likely. It is true that the member states have tended to consider that in many areas, their only capacity to have any kind of real independence after the loss of Great Power status was by co-operating with each other: they were unable to rival the powerful nations such as the USA or the Soviet Union on their own, and needed to collaborate in order to prevent relegation to the third division of states. Thus, integration in certain policy areas can be seen as the defence, or best use, of national sovereignty (Milward 1992; Moravcsik 1999). In this view, European states have more to gain than to lose by co-operating; but because the wish to preserve autonomy as far as possible remains powerful, they will continually police the progress of European integration, and ensure that it never reaches the point at which the member states are effectively redundant.

Given this general approach, it is not surprising that a further reason for the limited competences of the EU is the fact that all member states must agree to support the acquisition of new competences by the Union. This is a significant brake on the integration process, because it means that just one state can prevent a step towards the deepening of the integration process that all the others desire – at least in terms of primary legislation.[1] Moreover, the member states continue to give the EU a very small budget when compared either with their own resources or those of large multinational corporations such as Coca-Cola or Microsoft. Thus, in crude financial terms, there is a clear and important limit to what the EU can do. The member states continue to want different things from the EU, and also continue to have different views about what the goals and limits of European integration should be. As a consequence, adding to the EU's powers tends to take time, and reflects the capacity to create and exploit suitable opportunities rather than sustained and balanced development strategies (Cram 1997). It is important to remember that in this respect, the EU's own institutions can be as influential as national governments; the Commission has sometimes been particularly noteworthy in this regard (Ross 1995).

Member states' agreement to deepen the integration process – that is, to add to the EU's competences – tends to rely upon their perception of a common external threat to which they can respond more effectively together than on their own. These threats have, in the past, been primarily economic, given the defence role of the USA outlined above and the continued wish on the part of national governments to retain as much autonomy as possible. Thus, increased competition from the USA, Japan and South East Asia led the member states to set up the single market, in order to be able to improve their economic efficiency and afford protection to European industry from the difficulties of global competition (Sandholtz and Zysman 1989). Globalisation has been construed as a similar threat, and part of the rationale for measures such as the single currency (Rosamond 1999).

Another factor is at play here, however: member states must not only perceive a common threat and consider that they can respond to it more effectively together than in isolation. They must also agree on the approach to policy which is adopted. The primacy of neoliberalism in many member states during the 1980s and 1990s significantly coloured the EU response to economic competition and globalisation: the creation of a European market and currency, which would remove barriers to trade in Europe, strengthen the EU as a global economic player, and help the EU fit more neatly into the global capitalist economy. Neoliberalism did not favour a strong EU social policy or the development of a new federal state at EU level. Thus, issues of political belief and ideology can be as important as issues of state power and autonomy in explaining how and why the EU develops its competences in particular ways.

IV: POLICY STYLES

Before introducing the EU's main policies, it is worth introducing the concept of 'policy style'. This is because the approach to making policy that the EU has adopted has changed over time, as have the systems and procedures that it employs (see Chapter 3). Here, the most significant development to note is the apparent shift away from orthodox ways of making policy in favour of 'soft policy'. Thus, while the EU is adding to its range of competences, it is by no means apparent that this process will produce further steps towards either a European federation or detailed Union legislation that involves the full range of EU institutions in its making.

Helen Wallace (2000) has shown that the EU system has roughly five different approaches to policy making. These range from the original method, which favoured binding regulation and gave all meaningful power to the Council and Commission – an approach still used in agriculture policy today – via its adaptations to use directives rather than regulations, and to empower the EP, regional governments and actors outside the state, to the use of the EU as a regulator[2], and eventually to approaches that are qualitatively different because they rest on alternative views of how good (EU) policy can be made. These approaches reduce the importance of the EU as a provider of either regulations or detailed binding legislation. The first is co-ordination or benchmarking, when the EU acts as a forum in which member states can compare their approaches to policy-making and agree best practice – an example is employment policy. The second is what Wallace dubs 'intensive transgovernmentalism', a practice in which member states develop between themselves informal norms and rules of co-operation, which can be extensive but which fall outside the formal competence of the EU. This form of integration may lead to more orthodox methods of EU action (Wallace cites intergovernmental co-operation on issues of monetary policy as a good example), but they also reveal that when adding new and sensitive issues to the EU agenda, the member states may prefer to keep the power to decide what is to be done about them to themselves. These 'soft policy' approaches tend to favour the national governments, the European Council and the EU Council rather than the Commission or EP. They may also impose new, and often poorly-understood, burdens of coordination and joined-up working between the EU bodies and those of the member states. If not adequately addressed, these burdens have the capacity to make EU governance less, rather than more, effective (Jordan and Schout 2006).

V: KEY INTERNAL POLICIES OF THE EUROPEAN UNION: BRIEF GUIDES

In this final substantive section, I provide brief guides to the EU's principal policies. These guides serve to give the reader a solid understanding of the reasons for EU competence in a particular area. They also set out why and to what extent this competence has developed or changed over time. I do not claim that these guides are either definitive or all-encompassing.[3] For supplementary information, the reader is directed to the 'further reading' section at the end of the chapter.

The Single European Market (SEM)

Constructing a single market for the EU was one of the primary goals of European integration, because it was considered likely to produce significant economic growth. The Rome Treaty, in fact, set out the aim of establishing such a market, with no restrictions to trade and free movement of goods, services, capital and labour – the so-called 'four freedoms' of the EU. Large fines can be imposed for infringements of this legislation. The Commission's Directorate General for Competition, which works on these issues, has always been regarded as strong. Progress towards the SEM goal was nonetheless slow for many years, because the original approach that was adopted depended on harmonisation of trading standards for goods and services.

The attempt to harmonise untold numbers of goods and services proved impossible, because the mass of legislation and subsequent changes to production were simply too great. In its 1979 *Cassis-de-Dijon* ruling, however, the European Court of Justice provided the means to accelerate the process when it ruled that member states could not refuse access to their national markets to goods and services produced in other member states on the ground that they were of a different standard (Alter and Meunier-Aitsahalia 1994). Instead, member states had the right to insist that goods entering their markets met agreed minimum shared standards. This seemingly technical decision paved the way forward because it made the legislative task far easier, and hugely reduced the changes to production processes that would be required. Thus, the project of creating a SEM became feasible. It also gained renewed priority status as a result of the economic downturn experienced in Western Europe at the time. Significantly, the member governments, transnational businesses and the EU institutions could all agree that the creation of the single market was essential in order to make the member states economically competitive. This agreement was made easier by two factors. First, the emerging neoliberal consensus in the member states, which held that the key to economic growth was market liberalisation rather than **protectionism**. Second, the capacity of the then President of the Commission, Jacques Delors, to assemble and maintain a coalition of support for the project.

The SEA which set out the basis for the single market was also significant because it made the first important changes to the formal workings of the EU since its inception. As the price to pay for the single market, member states agreed to allow qualified majority voting in the Council on matters relating to the SEM so that no individual state could block progress. They also agreed to reform the EU's budget, and to tie the institutional reform into the process of enlarging the EU which had begun with the accession of Greece and was to continue with that of Portugal and Spain (Young and Wallace 2000).

Although the single market is still not entirely complete – as the controversy over the Services Directive in 2006 attests – there is no doubt that the project has on the whole been a great success, at least if we use as a yardstick member states' readiness to continue to abide, generally speaking, by its provisions. However, it is true that some of the 'flanking policies' necessary to its optimum functioning from a social democratic perspective are under-developed; social policy and personal freedom of movement are good examples.

Economic and monetary union (the single currency)

The single currency has also been a long-standing ambition of the EU, and was adopted as an explicit goal by the Hague Summit of 1969. For some proponents, a single currency would be the next step beyond a single market towards complete economic integration. For others, its advantages centred on making the most of the single market by making it cheaper and easier to trade between member states, and on increasing the strength of the EU vis-à-vis both global markets and the US dollar.

This ambition too, however, was fated to be beset by difficulties. Throughout the 1970s and 1980s, projects designed as initial steps towards a single currency fell apart, because in the absence of a single market the member states' economies were too divergent, and also because national governments were not yet prepared to abandon control of monetary policy (Lintner 2001). However, as part of the Maastricht Treaty, detailed plans for the adoption of the single currency were agreed in order to capitalise on the benefits of the single market and to take the integration process forward in the face of both the collapse of communism and German reunification (Pryce 1994). Efforts to co-ordinate monetary policies were stepped-up, and specific '**convergence criteria**' were established. Member states which wished to take part would need to demonstrate that they had an annual budget deficit of less than 3% of GDP and a maximum public sector debt of 60% of GDP. They would also need to prove they had maintained their fixed exchange rates against other member state currencies for 2 years, kept inflation to a level below 1.5% above the average rate of the three member states with the lowest inflation levels, and lowered interest rates to no more than 2% above the average of the three lowest-rate member states. The single currency was launched 'virtually' in 1999, replacing national currencies in all electronic transactions, and the euro replaced the national currencies of those member states which participated in 2002.

The single currency is now perhaps the flagship policy of the EU. It has provided the Union with a symbol and tangible product of integration, and, despite teething problems with the currency markets, has so far proved resilient. It is a major achievement, and at the time of writing is considered a stronger currency than the US dollar, judging by currency exchange rates. However, the euro remains controversial. The rules which were set up to govern it – the Stability and Growth Pact, attached to the Amsterdam Treaty – are increasingly considered to be too restrictive to allow national governments adequate leeway for intervention when their economies are in difficulty. They have also been completely ignored by France and Germany. Many observers also consider that the job of the European Central Bank – primarily to keep inflation very low – is too narrow, and that the ECB is too independent to allow democratic control of its actions. Several member states are outside the euro-zone by choice (Denmark, Sweden and the UK), although others must join as soon as they qualify (as indeed has happened with Slovenia, Cyprus and Malta). Furthermore, the redistributive policies of the EU have not been strengthened to match the EU's new competence in monetary policy, leading some to fear that the Union may exacerbate economic problems in particular regions or states even if its overall impact is positive. Indeed, it may also be that times of economic hardship such as those apparently prefaced as this book went to press may undermine the euro's success (Dyson 2008).

The Common Agricultural Policy (CAP)

The CAP was, together with competition policy, the great early success story of the EU. Established to ensure an adequate food supply for the member states and to protect EU farmers from overseas competition, it is based on the idea of market intervention – a fact which also denotes its role as an exception to the usual market logic of the EU. Essentially, the CAP guarantees farmers that the price paid for their produce will not fall below an agreed level, even if the world market price falls below it. Thus, farmers' incomes are subsidised, helping maintain a farming community in the Union and thereby guaranteeing that the EU can feed itself.

However, the CAP has become increasingly controversial, for a number of reasons. The first, perhaps, is its existence outside the normal EU approach of allowing market forces to rule (Rieger 2000): those operating in other sectors of the economy, and subject to the full forces of competition, increasingly fail to see why farmers should not face the same treatment. Those representing consumers argue that the CAP keeps prices artificially high because it shields the EU from global markets and cheaper food imports. Environmental groups oppose the CAP's tendency to encourage overproduction (the infamous food mountains and drink lakes), and to encourage industrial rather than organic farming. The US, the developing world and the **WTO** complain that the CAP discriminates against their own products – a wrong which is felt particularly acutely by developing countries. Still others point out that the CAP takes up almost half the EU budget; if the CAP were abolished, that money could be spent on other policies, such as regional cohesion or development. Thus, pressures for reform have been growing, and successive changes have been made to the CAP. In 2003, a further reform was brokered by Commissioner Fischler in the face of great opposition. Thus, it appears that the future CAP will be less deserving of criticism on the grounds of excessive production or unfair subsidy – a process that is likely to be reinforced by future agreements at the WTO, should the Doha Round of that organisations negotiations ever reach a conclusion.

Regional policy

Regional policy was established in order to help economically backward regions of the member states to develop. It is a further indicator of the EU's unique successes in developing as a political system, because it allows the transfer of resources between the member states on the ground that they have an obligation to reduce the gaps between the richer and poorer regions of the single market. Regional policy owes its place in the set of EU policies to three major factors. Two of these are ideological; one is hard-nosed national interest. On the ideological side, there are two key issues. First, the need to mitigate the impact of competition policy on regional development, because the EU's competition policy made state aids to such regions either difficult or impossible. Second, there is a perceived need to help even out the development potential of the Union's richer and poorer regions in order to gain optimal benefit from the single market. This kind of thinking encouraged the EU to develop a mechanism to transfer resources to its economically weakest regions – the 'cohesion policy' (Bache 1998; De Rynck and McAleavey 2001). On the national interest side, there is what Eiko Thielemann (2002) calls a 'compensation logic' in evidence. Member states which did not receive large payments under the CAP regime sought a means to demonstrate to their publics that membership of the EU had financial benefits and not just costs; they thus promoted the idea of regional policy as a *juste retour* or 'fair return' on the costs of EU membership.

This double rationale for EU regional policy has made its evolution difficult, because it has never been clear whether the policy is really about regional development in the EU's truly poorest areas or about allowing each member state a slice of the regional budget pie (Pollack 1995; Keating and Hooghe 2001). Nonetheless, a clear principle has been established in order to promote the involvement of

actors from regional/local government and civil society in the forma-
tion and implementation of regional policy: partnership. Additionally,
there is a norm which in theory ensures member state governments
match, and do not merely swallow up, whatever monies come back to
the regions from Brussels: additionality. Finally, a third double principle ensures that whatever projects are funded are efficiently targeted
and managed: programming and concentration.

There is no doubt that EU money has been a key factor in the success of many regeneration projects in the member states. However, it
is also clear that national governments have been keen to restrict the
development of partnerships at local or regional level, and they have
also often ignored the additionality principle (Bache 1998). Moreover,
although the proportion of the EU budget that is devoted to regional
policy has been growing, the actual sums of money involved remain
inadequate, given the small size of the EU budget itself. Thus, the
ability of EU regional policy to transform the developmental potential of its poorest regions must be open to question. This has recently
become even clearer because the pre-2004 member states have so far
failed both to increase their contributions to the EU budget and to
share regional policy money fairly with the 2004 and 2007 entrants,
all of which could make a better claim to it than the earlier EU members (Zielonka 2006).

Environmental policy

The EU's powers in this area of policy are intriguing, not least because
they arose without the benefit of an explicit Treaty basis. Before the
SEA provided this basis, the EU made environmental policy through
provisions on harmonious economic development and ensuring
decent standards of living (Marin 1997). Environmental policy's
other impressive features are its degree of supranationality, i.e. the
fact that the EU has a great deal of power in this area, and its part in
building up the Union's role in international politics (Warleigh 2003:
95). As always, the drive to create the SEM played a significant role
in the development of environment policy at the EU level. This is
partly shown by the remarks immediately above about the use of
economic development policy to enact environmental provisions.
It is also revealed by the determination of many member states with
advanced environmental legislation to ensure that the single market

did not put their companies at a disadvantage because they had to incorporate greater costs, and thus charge higher prices, than companies from less 'green' member states (Sbragia 2000).

However, in the case of environment policy, factors other than market-making were important. This is because, given the Union's general trend towards privileging market-making over market intervention, it would have been logical for the member states to remove barriers to competition by eradicating environmental policy (Marin 1997). Instead, they chose to set new common standards of environmental protection, which in many cases were far more stringent than national legislation in the area. This can be partially explained by the historical context of the single market: popular awareness of ecological problems was approaching its height in the mid- to late 1980s, and Union legislation in this area was considered likely to be popular. This was particularly probable given widespread acceptance of the truism that pollution knows no frontiers, and thus purely national action against environmental problems may be ineffective.

EU environment policy has established three core principles: prevention is better than cure, or the precautionary principle; those who pollute should be responsible for repairing the damage, or the 'polluter pays' principle; and all policy, not just that which is obviously environmental, must have no negative effect on the environment: the mainstreaming or integration principle. This is an impressive array of useful principles, and constitutes the basis for effective environmental policy, which is elaborated through a series of Environmental Action Programmes, or EAPs, the sixth of which lasts from 2002 to 2012.

EU environmental legislation has had many successes, and in many ways, such as the Emissions Trading Scheme developed to help reduce climate change, the EU has been innovative (if only partially successful). For example, it has contributed to improving standards of drinking and bathing water, reducing air pollution, and ensuring that major development projects such as roads comply with agreed standards of environmental protection. However, the content of environment policy is frequently decided as a result of political bargains and deliberation rather than as a result of adherence to clear scientific principles, because the issues at stake are economically costly. Thus, Union policy is often less ecologically sound when it reaches the statute book after a difficult journey down the policy chain than when it was initially envisaged and proposed. Moreover, there is a significant problem of non-implementation of environment policy, because member states wish to avoid the often significant costs of complying with the legislation (Barnes and Barnes 1999).

Perhaps more importantly, there are also continuing difficulties with mainstreaming environmental issues into other policy areas. The Treaty now makes sustainable development – i.e. environmentally friendly economic growth – a core objective of the Union. However, precisely how this goal is to be achieved is less than clear, and sectors of national governments, the Commission and the EP with no direct interest in environmentalism often frustrate mainstreaming in order to protect their own interests. Given the tendency towards 'soft policy' outlined in Section IV earlier, it is also unclear whether mainstreaming environmental policy is realistic under the current dynamics of the EU system (Jordan and Schout 2006).

Social policy

Union social policy has tended to focus on labour-related and gender equality issues, taking as its starting point the Treaty provisions on single market. It has produced several impressive directives, not to mention ECJ rulings, notably in the areas of gender equality at work, health and safety at work, and access to welfare payments for member state nationals when residing in member states other than their own. However, it has failed to replicate the depth and breadth of national social policies in Western Europe. This is because the EU's relative stagnation of the 1970s was overcome not by European-level **social democracy**, which would have placed the accent on social policy, but by a largely neoliberal project of market-making which, in the words of the then UK Prime Minister Margaret Thatcher, considered that there was no such thing as society.

As an accompaniment to the single market, Commission President Delors advocated a Social Charter, which was again primarily focused on the workplace. However, the UK strongly resisted the development of EU social policy, securing the right to opt out of any measures proposed under the Social Charter, and the other member states adopted the latter in non-binding form only (Dinan 1999). The Social Protocol attached to the Maastricht Treaty was theoretically an advance, but it too remained non-binding. Moreover, the Commission was wary about proposing radical measures in social policy given the stiffness of UK resistance; it was only with the Amsterdam Treaty that the UK, with its then newly-elected Labour government, withdrew its opt-out from certain aspects of EU social policy. However, since Amsterdam the climate has remained difficult for social policy because, in the approach to the launch of the euro, most of the member states were under severe restraints in their public spending. This trend appears even more significant when it is remembered that many member states have used the SEM and the euro as reasons to dismantle national social policies, without introducing equivalent legislation at the EU level (Scharpf 1999). As indicated by the debates over the Treaty of Lisbon, the neoliberal/social democrat argument remains sharp: the UK insisted on reducing the scope of the EU's social policies, yet France insisted on a protocol which states the EU must do more to promote social justice.

According to some observers, the EU's social policy really owes more to the judgements of the ECJ than to the member states (Leibfried and Pierson 2000). The Court may or may not be deliberately activist, but many of its rulings advance the reach of EU social policy on an ad hoc basis through such judgements as *Cowan*, which ruled that tourists in member states other than their own have the right to receive criminal injury compensation as if they were nationals of that state. Thus, it could be argued that although EU social policy is not as extensive as many on the left of the political spectrum might wish, it has made more of an impact on the lives of EU citizens than may be immediately apparent. It may also be, despite the political football played with the so-called 'European Social Model', which pits defenders of an active social policy for the EU against those who see it in more market-driven terms, that there is at least some shared notion of the EU's role in this area, and even of how this could link to its external identity (Delanty and Rumford 2005). It should also be remembered that there is currently much Union activity in the social policy realm in the form of soft policy, such as co-ordinating action to combat unemployment.

VI: CONCLUSIONS

The EU's internal, or domestic, policies can thus be considered extensive. Although the principal focus of the EU has changed over time, in response to both internal factors, i.e. those originating in the member states, *and* external factors, it has charted a course towards the acquisition of an impressive range of competences. Although these are often focused on trade and economics, such as the single market or the euro, they can also be a means by which markets are regulated, such as competition policy, or even bucked – for example, the CAP. Thus, although the main internal policy successes of the Union are often considered to be economic in nature, it would be a mistake to consider the Union as an also-ran in other policy areas – not least because the single market in particular can often have what may be unintended consequences for a whole range of policies, ranging from environmental protection to public health.

Over time, the EU has developed powers in an increasing range of issue areas, to the extent that in 2008 no member state of the Union is really sovereign any longer in the orthodox Westphalian sense, if indeed they ever were. That said, there are also clear limits to the competences of the EU. Although these too can and do change, it is apparent that where member states wish to keep an area of policy outside the EU's portfolio of responsibilities, they can to a very great extent do so via the unanimity rule on Treaty change – as demonstrated amply by the UK's insistence on several 'red lines' during the negotiations that led up to the Treaty of Lisbon.

The ways in which the EU functions – its policy styles – are also worthy of attention. These have developed in a way which gives member states maximum freedom of manoeuvre even while the EU acts in an increasing number of policy areas – not only through its emphasis on directives rather than regulations, as discussed in Chapter 3, but also through its increasing use of soft policy. Such developments reinforce the view that the EU and its member states are not really capable of a clear distinction between them; if the EU is increasingly the venue in which so-called national policies are made, it remains dependent upon its member states for their execution.

THINK POINTS

- To what extent, and why, have the powers of the EU increased over time?
- Why has the single market played such a key role in defining what the EU does, and does not, do?

- Why has the EU turned increasingly to soft policy? Is this a good thing?
- Do you think the EU should increase or decrease its range of policies? If so, which ones, and why?

FURTHER READING

Cini, Michelle (ed.) (2006) *European Union Politics* (2nd edn) (Oxford: Oxford University Press).
An up-to-date textbook which includes chapters on several of the EU's major policies.

Jordan, Andrew and Schout, Adriaan (2006) *The Coordination of the European Union: Exploring the Capacities for Networked Governance* (Oxford: Oxford University Press).
An impressive volume exploring the EU's recent experiments with different policy styles and mechanisms, with particular reference to environment policy.

Marks, Gary, Scharpf, Fritz, Schmitter, Philippe and Streeck, Wolfgang (1996) *Governance in the European Union* (London: Sage).
An intriguing mix of conceptual and empirical articles exploring the extent to which the EU has gone beyond market-based integration with specific reference to social policy.

Scharpf, Fritz (1999) *Governing in Europe: Effective and Democratic?* (Oxford: Oxford University Press).
A very impressive analysis of the market-making as a tool of European integration and its impact on governance at both national and EU levels.

Wallace, Helen, Wallace, William and Pollack, Mark (eds) (2006) *Policy-Making in the European Union* (5th edn) (Oxford: Oxford University Press).
An excellent set of essays explaining the main developments and dilemmas of a range of EU policies.

THE EUROPEAN UNION IN THE WORLD

INTRODUCTION

One of the most striking and controversial aspects of European integration is the way in which the European Union (EU) has come to have its own external policies. In other words, in some policy issues it is the EU itself, rather than its member states, which is responsible for engaging with third countries and deciding their relationship to the member states as a collective. This is striking because it is without parallel in contemporary global politics: although there are powerful global institutions such as the WTO, they cannot by definition have an external policy while we still cannot be sure there are lifeforms elsewhere than on this planet. Other regional groupings, such as **ASEAN**, do have external policies of a kind, but they cannot match the EU for its breadth and depth of competence in this regard. This role for the EU is controversial because it can pose a threat to member state sovereignty in one of its core characteristics, namely the ability of a state to determine how it engages with the outside world.

Of course, it would be a mistake to exaggerate the powers of the EU to shape world politics, or to replace the role of its member states as a foreign policy actor. As this chapter will show, there are many clear limitations to the powers of the EU in this regard, and it is not clear whether these gaps will, or even should, ever be filled (Hill 1995).

Moreover, the EU is an actor of a particular kind on the world stage: it has very little military capacity, and none of the little that it has is independent, as it depends on both its member states and NATO. Instead, the EU tends to rely on its economic power and diplomacy to shape world politics, although it has also been able to deploy an increasing range of other policy instruments as well. In this chapter, I set out why the EU has an external policy capacity of its own, and investigate some of the principal ways in which this action capacity has been understood by commentators. I then look at the role the EU plays in external policy in three main areas: economic diplomacy, development aid, and defence and security policy. I address the issue of the EU's role in stabilising its neighbourhood through preparing candidate countries for accession – the enlargement process – under this heading. This has been a key, and so far highly successful, aspect of the EU's external policy.

The core argument of the chapter is that the EU's powers in external policy are extensive. In some policy issues, the EU has effectively replaced member states as the means by which they engage with the external world, for example in world trade negotiations or those on global environmental policy, although of course what this really means is that the EU is the device by which member states coordinate their negotiation strategies to increase their diplomatic power. The EU's external powers can be understood to decline, relatively speaking, as we move from economic diplomacy to the military aspects of security, but this balance of competences is shifting; while the EU may never have a standing army of its own it is certainly increasingly able to play a role in security and peacekeeping operations outside its borders. Moreover, the increasing importance of non-military instruments of external policy, such as economic diplomacy, means that the EU's relative lack of capacity in this regard should not be taken to indicate low influence in global politics – a point to which I return below.

WHY THE EU HAS ITS OWN EXTERNAL POLICY

One of the striking things about the EU's external capacity is what it reveals about the changing role of the nation state, or at least those which have joined the Union, at the turn of the twenty-first century. Member state foreign policy now has to coexist with that of the

EU (Smith 2004); and, although this should not be exaggerated, participation in the EU changes a member state's interaction not just with its fellow members but with third countries. True, there is no EU foreign ministry; however, if it is ratified the Lisbon Treaty will enhance the Union's institutional capacity and give it an External Action Service, a move which would make the Union's external policy role rather more explicit.

To some extent, this role of the Union can be seen as simply logical. If states erect a customs union between themselves, for example, and attach to that a common tariff for goods from third countries seeking to enter that customs union area, at the very least they will have to coordinate their monitoring and policing of that tariff. This has been the case for the EU since the 1950s. Furthermore, if that customs union deepens, and becomes a single market, then global trade politics will require the common articulation of the collective interests of that common market – it would make no sense to have, for example, Slovakia, Spain and Sweden all trying to argue different positions at the WTO. Indeed, it is relationships with that single market – or access to it – that third countries often want, and clearly this cannot be in the gift of any single member state, but must rather be a collective decision. Thus, the EU, which in this case means the Commission, negotiates trade matters concerning access to the EU market with, for example, China, although of course individual member states also develop particular relationships with Beijing.

However, beyond this kind of economic policy and trade politics role, the EU's external policies are not so easy to explain as simply the result of the EU's own economic integration. Instead, the other major roles played by the EU beyond its borders are better explained by deliberate member state choice to pool their sovereignty in this way, in order to achieve more of their objectives through collective action than they could in all probability achieve on their own. The EU is increasingly the device by which the member states interact with global politics, as it can be a means of drawing a veil over a difficult relationship between one member state and the third country in question, or by which as a group, or sub-group, the member states have something credible to offer or withhold from a third country: for example, the EU's ongoing diplomacy with Iran, led by Germany, France and the UK, is often more successful than the more heavy-handed US approach. It can be cheaper to act together, or to allow one member state to act for another – for instance, one of the rights of EU citizenship is the right of any EU citizen to seek diplomatic protection from another member state if her own does not have an embassy or consulate in the country in which she is travelling. Thus, to take a hypothetical example, a Frenchwoman in difficulties in Mongolia could demand assistance from the Finnish embassy in the absence of a diplomatic presence from Paris in Ulan Bator.

Geopolitical factors also shape the development of external policy capacity by the EU. For example, the attitude of the USA is often crucial in determining whether and how the EU develops competence in a particular issue, especially in matters of defence and security. Thus, the role of the USA in both pushing for European integration, but seeking to restrain the ability of the EU to develop an independent military capacity which Washington could not at least co-shape, has been extremely important. This has made Washington a Janus-faced factor in the evolution of EU external policy capacity; by providing Western European security during the Cold War via NATO, the USA arguably facilitated the development of EU economic power, but it has also, by insisting on yoking the EU's small, but growing, military role to NATO, placed a clear limit on the evolution of that role. In recent years, when EU–US tensions, or at least tensions between the USA and many of the EU's member states, have often been acute, this continuing role for NATO in European defence has been increasingly controversial (Pond 2004). The waters are muddied even more by the reliance of many in the USA foreign policy establishment on the development by the EU of at least some degree of independent defence/military capacity, in order for the Union to be able to deal with problems in its 'neighbourhood' and thereby free up Washington's resources for deployment elsewhere (Calleo 2001). This tension is also reflected in the attitude towards EU external policy, particularly in security and defence issues, of its member states: as an illustration, the UK has traditionally been Atlanticist, seeing the EU as the USA's potential junior partner, but France has traditionally been quite happy to envisage an independent Europe.

Additionally, there is a role for ideology in helping explain the development of the EU's powers in external policy. The EU was given the task of achieving 'ever closer union' between its member states. If that is to be taken seriously, clearly issues of external policy must at some point enter into the mix. This is not just because there is not always a neat division between 'the domestic' and 'the international' – most issues in contemporary politics involve significant cross-border flows of some kind. For example, the EU's common agricultural policy reform process, a seemingly 'internal' issue for the Union and its member states, must be undertaken in full view of the EU's relations with the developing world and in the context of the evolving global trade regime (Piening 1997). We must also pay attention to EU external policy because, as mentioned above, control of this issue area is traditionally understood as a core aspect of national sovereignty, and thus, if those who are critical of the EU may want to limit its external policy role on that ground, for the very same reasons those who advocate closer integration will tend to want to strengthen this role. Thus, one of the most significant aspects of the Maastricht Treaty was often held to be its creation of the so-called 'second pillar' of Union activity, which pledged the EU to a common foreign and security policy, the **CFSP**. This policy was explicitly described as having the potential to produce, in time, a common EU defence. The fact that this 'pillar' of the EU has nonetheless remained almost entirely the preserve of the member states, with no authoritative role for the Commission, European Parliament, or the ECJ, shows the dilemma very clearly: are the member states really ready to pool that much sovereignty, and if not, is it really feasible to bracket off some areas of 'foreign policy' from others to which they are increasingly related?

WHAT KIND OF FOREIGN POLICY ACTOR IS THE EU?

When we speak of EU external policy it is ultimately, in fact, the collective policy of its member states. In other words, the Union is *both* a system of international relations in its own right, i.e. relations between its member states, *and* an actor in broader international/ global politics (Hill and Smith 2005b). It is a means by which its member states both work with each other and, as a group, engage with the rest of the world. This means that the Union is unlikely to match powerful individual states in terms of its external policy decision-making processes or perceived independence. It also means that the Union must develop its external policies, as indeed is the case for its internal policies, through a process of complex negotiation and bargaining, both between its member states and between its supranational-level institutions.

Furthermore, the EU has different powers and is represented by different actors/institutions depending on the external policy issue in question. For example, in external trade negotiations, the Commission plays a highly significant role, negotiating on behalf of the member states and often demonstrating a degree of independence in this regard (Hix 2005: 382). In issues of non-trade diplomacy, however, it is often the High Representative – currently Javier Solana – who will represent the Union, sometimes accompanied by, or even replaced by, representatives from the so-called Big Three: France, Germany and the UK. This increases the difficulty of coordination in the EU, but reflects the collective will of the member states regarding how far they are prepared to delegate their autonomy to the EU at a given point in time.

BOX 5.1: EUROPE AS GLOBAL POWER OR GLOBAL ALSO-RAN?

In recent years, the future role of the EU in global politics has been debated vigorously. Among the many useful contributions, two are outlined here because they take diametrically opposed views. Mark Leonard (2005) argues that the EU is an example of how politics is changing in an era of globalisation. As states become more and more dependent upon each other, and on international rules, the use of force as an instrument of foreign policy is becoming less and less viable. The EU has a head start in understanding this situation, which reflects how it has worked for over fifty years. Blessed with this experience, the Union has an innate understanding of how to make contemporary global politics work, and is likely to do so more effectively than other players like the USA, whose understandings of how influence is exercised are old-fashioned. Indeed, for Leonard, the EU is a model of how states should organise themselves in the twenty-first century, and is increasingly recognised as such by other global regions.

A different perspective is put forward by Robert Kagan (2004). He argues that the EU's formal limitations as a collective of independent states rather than a state in its own right doom it to playing a minor role in world affairs. For Kagan, being a major power ultimately requires the ability to use force aggressively, even as a last resort. The EU cannot do this, and has no realistic prospect of being able to, because its member states will not sacrifice that much sovereignty: if a European army were created, it would require the creation of an EU state, and this would be, for Kagan, like turkeys voting for Christmas. Instead, the EU and its member states will continue to depend on the USA to provide their security, and will simply have to put up with being at best its junior partner, accepting Washington's priorities as the price to be paid for protection under its security umbrella.

There are two basic positions regarding the significance of the EU's external policy role. The first argues that the EU is riding the wave of the future, and is well on the way to being the kind of player that will dominate world affairs in the twenty-first century (e.g. Leonard 2005). The second argues that the EU is doomed to play a marginal role in global affairs, since it is much weaker than the USA, which has shaped the international system to suit its own interests, and the Union's member states will never cede as much sovereignty to the EU as would be necessary to develop a European army that could rival those of other powers (Kagan 2004). In a way, both perspectives are right: the EU is adroit at playing the complex games of global economic diplomacy and negotiations, but it also has clear military weaknesses and cannot use a credible threat of force to impose its will on third countries. Thus, one's view of the EU's ability to act meaningfully on the world stage is to a great extent dependent upon what one considers necessary for any actor to do this; if military power is crucial for global significance, then the EU is marginalised, but if military power is not so necessary then there is scope for the Union's perceived role to grow.

The key debate here thus focuses on whether the Union can, or should, exert meaningful influence over the affairs of third countries and international organisations through means other than the threat or use of violence. The best expression of this in the contemporary literature is the idea of 'normative power Europe' (Manners 2002;

BOX 5.2: NORMATIVE POWER EUROPE

Manners' 2002 article, which first argued that the EU is a normative power, has received much attention from both scholars and policy-makers. In essence, Manners argues that the EU has always preferred to used civilian tools of foreign policy (economic diplomacy, development aid, **technical transfer** etc), and that this is as much the result of deliberate choice as of lack of alternatives. This thinking has been carried through from the days when the EU had no military capacity at all to more recent years, where this capacity has begun to be acquired. In other words, the EU is, for Manners, an unusual kind of external policy actor, not just because of its novel structures, but because of the way this leads it to understand the best way to approach global politics: through supporting the creation of a rule-based, multilateral world order, and by using its economic powers to promote economic stability, economic growth and good governance where it can. The EU will, in this view, also use whatever military capacity it has or acquires to back-up this general stance, by using its military wing for only peace-keeping and humanitarian missions.

see Box 5.2). From this perspective, the Union is deemed able to wield enormous influence in world affairs by employing such tools as a generous development policy, **conditionality** in its aid agreements and policy over access to its internal market to promote reform of others' policies and structures, and playing a key role in the development of a more multi-lateral, rule-bound world. This kind of emerging global governance structure is seen to reflect the Union's own identity – the claim is that the EU has a kind of ethical foreign policy that results from its own role as a means to bring peace and stability to its member states through trade and submission to new collective rules and institutions (Bretherton and Vogler 2006). Although the EU is developing a military capacity, this remains small and limited to the so-called **Petersberg Tasks** of peace-keeping and humanitarian intervention, which are increasingly called-for in a world where armed conflict is generally seen as an illegitimate way of solving problems (issues in the Persian Gulf and Middle East notwithstanding). From a 'normative power' perspective, therefore, the Union is capable of impacting upon the world stage in a range of effective ways.

Sceptics of the 'normative power' perspective argue that it is largely window-dressing, i.e. it makes a virtue of necessity by 'bigging up' the EU in a way which makes it appear more relevant than it really is (Kagan 2004). Furthermore, it must be open to question just how far the EU is 'normative' in its use of power; it may prefer to use non-military instruments, but does that mean the EU is any less devoted to pursuit of its own interests than other actors in the international system?

The following sections of the chapter briefly sketch the three main areas of EU external policy – economic diplomacy, development policy, and security and defence – in order to shed some light on these issues.

ECONOMIC DIPLOMACY – TRADE POLITICS AND GLOBAL NEGOTIATIONS

In this chapter I use the term 'economic diplomacy' to refer to the EU's use of its economic power as a tool to secure the outcomes it wants in its relations with third countries. Thus, the term covers a range of activities from negotiations over trade policy at the WTO to the EU's participation in global fora such as UN summits on climate change, where its influence is largely derived from its wealth and market power, as well, perhaps, as its negotiating skill, reputation and substantive proposals. Although enlargement of the Union is arguably a form of economic diplomacy, it is also a form of security policy, and I follow Smith (2004) in categorising it in this way. Hence, a discussion of enlargement is to be found later in the chapter. I also treat development policy separately since, although it is intimately connected to the EU's market power, it is subject to different policy dynamics, decision rules and pressures.

The Union's economic power is potentially enormous. With twenty-seven member states, the Union spans almost the entire continent of Europe, which is both densely populated and wealthy by world standards. The single market has enabled the EU to harness its wealth more effectively, both domestically, by helping to increase GDP of the member states, and externally, by acting as a magnet that attracts foreign companies and governments eager for the wealth that can be generated from trading with and in such a vast market. The single currency enables the Union, or at least those of its member states in the euro-zone, to present a united front against global speculators, and could also enable the Union to constitute a rival or alternative **global reserve currency** to the US dollar.

In global trade negotiations, the EU is able to play a key role in shaping the development of new regulations. It is also powerful enough to resist significant pressure for change, for example over ending the protection of its agricultural sector. Together with the USA, it has conventionally been viewed as a key power at the WTO and its predecessor, GATT. The Union is therefore often a source of attraction for third countries, who may seek to use it to persuade the USA to change its policies and requirements; it is also a force to be reckoned with by the USA, which must either work with the Union to develop compromises or run the risk of failure (Baldwin *et al.* 2003). This does not add up to independent power for the EU: to achieve its objectives at the WTO, it will also need to find compromises with Washington and other third countries. There are times when the EU and the USA prefer to cooperate against the interests of the developing countries, as shown by the difficulties of the Doha round of WTO negotiations. Nonetheless, the Union is clearly a major power in matters of global trade politics; furthermore, it is capable of using its market access rules, and its right to decide market access privileges for third country companies, as a tool of foreign policy – as several high-profile American-based multinationals, such as Microsoft, have discovered to their cost.

The EU's economic power can also lend it credibility in other global negotiations. For example, the **Kyoto Protocol** on combating climate change was ultimately dependent upon the EU to drive the international agreement in the face of the USA's initial truculence and then outright opposition (Damro and Mendéz 2003). Although much of the key for success here was diplomatic credibility and skill, the EU's ability to assume the leadership role and be accepted by third countries in this capacity was due in great part to its claim to leadership legitimacy, which is in turn linked to its economic power. This link was deepened because the EU's readiness to consider at least some degree of economic reform, and responsibility to help developing countries develop sustainably, made it a credible advocate of the use of economic tools to solve a range of policy problems. This does, of course, also impact upon the EU's capacity to claim 'normative power' status, a claim which is arguably deepened in the wake of its stewardship of the Bali Climate Change Summit in 2007.

DEVELOPMENT POLICY

When advocates of a greater role for the EU in world politics want to marshal supporting evidence for the claim that this would be useful, they will often point to development policy to demonstrate what the Union can do when it acts in a unified way. Certainly, the EU gives a great deal of aid to developing countries; indeed, by many reckonings, when the EU is taken together with its individual member states, it is the world's biggest aid giver, contributing 51% of the world aid total (Bretherton and Vogler 2006). As a consequence, the Union has unquestionably carved out a niche for itself as a relatively generous Western power. However, it is worth exploring why this is, and evaluating the extent to which the Union's development policy is seen as an untrammelled success by the recipients of its aid.

Created early in the integration process, EU development policy owes its origins to the fact that several of the member states were in the process of retreating from imperial status, i.e. they were leaving their erstwhile colonies, which were embarking on the difficult journey to viable statehood. This meant that member states had long-established links and connections in the developing world that they wanted to preserve, and also that in some cases they were dependent upon such countries for certain natural resources or other aspects of trade. Thus, the bulk of EU development aid has gone to countries in Africa and the Caribbean/Pacific region, the so-called **ACP** states, and owes as much to enlightened self-interest as to idealism.

Similarly, EU development policy was established with the claims that it would be of mutual benefit to both the donors and the recipients, and that it would be elaborated in a spirit of genuine collaboration (Piening 1997). However, over time this claim has been increasingly contested, with questions often asked regarding whether the Union is really any different from any other aid donor regarding its wish to use such money to secure its own priorities through imposing conditionality on aid (Smith 2007). Certainly, developing countries often register concerns regarding the rolling out of EU aid policy; indeed, early concepts of EU–ACP partnership have often appeared to be losing ground to a less symmetrical relationship, one based on terms increasingly imposed by the EU (Bretherton and Vogler 2006). This change can largely be attributed to the shift in the West towards neoliberal economic models since the 1980s, which argue that economic development in the third world is more likely to arise from the establishment of the right kind of state structure – 'good governance', and a shift in the balance of power between the state and the market in favour of the latter – than from other forms of subsidy or support. However, power politics has also played a role, with the EU member states often eager to protect their domestic interest groups and industries rather than delivering entirely upon their pro-global poor rhetoric (Meunier and Nicolaïdis 2006: 918–22).

However, for all its shortcomings, the EU remains a key actor in development policy, and is much more generous than any other actor in this regard, although China has recently developed some interesting no-strings forms of aid policy to several African states, in return for preferential access to natural resources. Arguably, if it did not insist on at least certain forms of conditionality, the Union would be giving away 'free money' without helping improve basic human rights or governance structures in developing countries. This would not help the living conditions of such countries' citizens much, and would erode the EU's claims to be a normative power. Such arguments must therefore be included in a balanced critique of EU development policy.

SECURITY AND DEFENCE POLICY

The EU's powers in security and defence policy are perhaps its most remarkable of all. This is not to say that they are its most extensive powers. They are not. But their existence and growth over time indicate that the EU has had a significant impact on its member states, not just in terms of how they relate to each other, but also regarding how they choose to exercise their respective powers in the wider world. As stated above, external policy is a classic feature of national sovereignty; the fate of the European Defence Community, proposed and narrowly rejected in 1954, seemed to confirm that what we now call the EU would be largely irrelevant in such matters. And yet, foreign ministries of member states routinely work together and send staff to work in each other's teams (Carlsnaes 2007). Moreover, the

EU is beginning to acquire a meaningful, if small, military role, focused on the Petersberg tasks, and if it is ratified the Lisbon Treaty will take the process of integration in these policy areas rather further, by establishing more complete structures and institutions at the EU level.

How has this come to pass? The path has been arduous, and progress is still limited. However, the need to defend their joint economic interests, especially in the context of the customs union and then the single market, have pushed the member states to develop joint mechanisms of broader external policy despite the remaining divergences in their respective national interests in global politics (George 1996; Piening 1997). Thus, the process of 'European Political Co-operation' was established in the 1970s, and by the 1980s had become tasked with going beyond member state consultation with each other about their individual foreign policies to the declared aim of establishing the so-called 'joint actions', i.e. common policies regarding events beyond the EU borders. Opinion is divided on the success of the EPC: for Nuttall (1992), it was feeble, and yet George (1996) argues despite its failure to develop into a full-blown common policy it did help the member states develop joint policies on issues such as the Euro-Arab Dialogue, not to mention bloc voting in the UN.

The Maastricht Treaty established the Common Foreign and Security Policy of the Union. Although this was deliberately kept separate from the existing EU policies, and the member states retained all power for themselves in this issue area by legally excluding the Commission, EP and ECJ from decision-making, it was at least a symbolic indication that further developments were possible. Progress was quickened by the St Malo agreement between the UK and French governments in 1998. This pledged the two states to cooperate increasingly in matters of defence, and to facilitate through this the further elaboration of a common European defence and security policy, albeit one which would be compatible with NATO. This declaration signalled the willingness to cooperate of the EU's two biggest military powers, and as a result it created the proverbial window of opportunity, driven by UK interests in finding a way that would alleviate the pressure from other states over London's non-participation in the euro (Dover 2006), and also by concerns that the EU was ill-equipped to manage some of the worst problems caused by the collapse of communism in the former Yugoslavia.

Developments came in the typical crab-like and gradual fashion of the EU, with partial upgrades over the following decade or so via the Treaties of Amsterdam and Nice. By 2000, the EU had established a High Representative for the CFSP and a staff unit to improve policy planning in this issue area (the Policy Unit). The Nice Treaty even expanded this unit to incorporate military staff, and by 2000 the EU had an identifiable 'European Security and Defence Policy' (ESDP) composed of the Petersberg Tasks, a planned Rapid Reaction Force drawing on military personnel from its member states, subsequently changed to the ominously-titled but rather smaller 'battle groups', and a range of civilian measures centred on using member state police, lawyers, administrators and other experts to bolster civil protection, police cooperation and the effective rule of law in third countries. The EU has since undertaken high-profile missions of this kind in the former Yugoslavia and Africa. Moreover, the High Representative has often proved an effective diplomat, and the EU's contribution to resolving certain ongoing diplomatic crises has often been considered productive (Bretherton and Vogler 2006).

On the negative side of the balance sheet, the development of an EU foreign and security policy has been hampered by the split between member states over major global issues such as the 'war on terror' and the Second Gulf War/War on Iraq. These divisions have often been deeply bitter and very stark; the UK and Poland, for example, supported the US-led invasion of Iraq, but other key EU states, such as France and Germany, most certainly did not. These divisions have demonstrated how hard it still is in some cases for the member states to develop joint views on important global issues. This serves as a reminder that whatever quiet progress is made behind the scenes in EU external policy, there is still some way to go before its member states routinely arrive at the same choice regarding the options in major foreign policy issues, and must be recalled in any balanced assessment of the EU's external policy capacity.

Perhaps, then, it is no surprise that the EU has had more success in perhaps its most innovative security policy – enlargement. The very use of enlargement as a security policy, one of course dependent upon 'soft' tools such as conditionality and monetary aid to promote governance or economic reform, reveals something about the EU's foreign policy roles and uniqueness – no state would routinely contemplate bringing neighbours peacefully within its borders, often at their own request, with the policy seen on both sides as a key guar-antee of the acceding states' stability and security, which in turn adds to that of the Union. Yet the Union has done this on six occasions so far, and is likely to do so again in the future.

Smith (2004) argues that enlargement has been a means by which the EU has deliberately developed its more general capacity in exter-nal policy, by developing new instruments and ideas that are portable across issue areas within the external policy domain. The member states have remained key in the creation of this policy – a European *Ostpolitik* in Smith's terms – but no single state has dominated, and the EU institutions, particularly the Commission, have also played a central role. In this way, perhaps, the EU's successful experience of enlargement may demonstrate both its impressive capacities and its limits as an external policy actor: promoting reform in a third country which wants what the Union can offer – membership, and hence full access to the single market and other EU policies – is a very particular circumstance, as the Union cannot offer membership to every third country with which it has to deal: could, for example, Israel or Libya join a 'European' Union? Indeed, even when membership is a realistic prospect, the EU's influence is not always as great as expected thanks to its own internal shortcomings, such as unclear and unevenly under-stood accession processes in the existing member states, and occasional inability effectively to track/enforce implementation of the *acquis* in applicant states (Grabbe 2006). That said, enlargement has so far been a great success for the Union, and as such it is an indication that non-military tools in external policy can certainly be effective.

CONCLUSIONS: NORMATIVE POWER EUROPE?

How can the overall role of the EU in external policy be understood? Is it accurate to understand the EU as a 'normative power'? For this to be true, the EU must both have meaningful powers in external policy, and seek to use them in a way which is guided by norms (or values) rather than simply interests or calculations about maximis-ing short-term gain.

Clearly, the picture is varied in terms of where power lies. In some aspects of external policy, it is the EU, and particularly the Commission, which has the primary role – this is, for example, the case in external trade policy, although it must be remembered that the member states establish the remit for the Commission here. In other issue areas, the

EU has mixed competence with the member states – for example, development policy. In still other areas of policy, the EU as such remains fairly powerless, if by 'the EU' we mean either the roles of supranational institutions or the degree to which power has formally shifted from member state capitals to Brussels. This would clearly be the case for defence and security policy, with the important exception of enlargement, in which EU institutions play a significant role, and where the EU has sole competence for obvious reasons: it would be impossible to have some member states allowing a third country to join, but others refusing to do so! The picture is made more complex still by the fact that the EU is increasingly active in international diplomacy; as well as the obvious failures to present a united front, e.g. the War on Iraq, there are many quieter successes, and many instances where it is the added value of the EU as a means to coordinate the work of its member states which adds to their power. This has been true, for example, of global negotiations about environmental policy in recent years. Overall, then, the EU has many important functions in external policy, and is certainly a major force to be reckoned with in many aspects of global affairs: it may not be a foreign policy power in the classical understanding of the Westphalian state, but it certainly has important foreign policy *powers* (Hill and Smith 2005a). It is also considered as a leader in global politics by many third countries, even if by the same token it cannot always live up to their expectations (Hill 1995; Elgström 2007).

Just how 'normative' an actor is the EU though? Arguably many actors in global politics are normative – the USA under George W. Bush could be considered normative in its pursuit of a certain idea of world politics and America's role in it. Norms are not neutral: being a 'normative actor' does not automatically make that actor one of the 'good guys'. However, the implication of the normative power Europe thesis is *both* that the EU tends to act in accordance with a guiding set of norms, *and* that these norms are politically more progressive than the alternatives offered by other global actors. Does this hold water?

A single chapter such as this cannot provide a definitive answer to this question, but it can point to helpful preliminary conclusions. On the sceptical side, it should be noted that the EU is completely capable of putting its own interests first, and is often quite as mean in its treatment of the developing world in WTO negotiations as, for example, the USA. Similarly, the development of the single market and single currency are arguably not primarily focused on creating a

multilateral world for its own sake, but rather on creating a multilateral world in which the EU remains a key player. Moreover, enlargement of the EU is a tool that has been selectively applied: for instance, Turkey has been waiting to join for roughly 40 years, and the argument that inclusion in the EU would bolster domestic reform arguably applies there more than anywhere. However, the enlargements of 2004, and especially 2007, demonstrated that states can join the EU before they have really made the transition to **liberal democracy**, and yet Turkey is still waiting on the outside.

On the advocatory side, the EU *does* privilege the use of instruments other than violence to achieve its objectives. It also pays regular attention to its norms of multilateralism and rule-based international/ global governance, and tends to pay much greater heed to international law and legal institutions than other global powers. Although its development policies may not be as generous or as free of strings as third world states would like, the EU, together with its member states, does donate more aid than any other actor, and thus goes further to putting its money where its mouth is than any other global player. Enlargement has been a means whereby many European states have either adjusted more effectively to globalisation (Sweden) or loss of empire/Great Power status (UK). It has also been a means whereby other states have discovered effective sovereignty (Ireland) or joined the family of modern democracies after emerging from dictatorship (Spain, Portugal, Greece). In global negotiations over climate change, the EU is clearly a force for good; again, it has not so far achieved as strict a policy regime as climate scientists tell us we need, but without the EU and its efforts there would be no Kyoto agreement and no 'Bali roadmap' either. This is a normative role for the EU insofar as it deepens the global multilateral order and helps promote sustainable development, to which the Union claims to be devoted.

Thus, on balance, the EU can indeed be seen as a normative power. It does not always act in keeping with its norms. It is not always particularly powerful. However, both in the instruments it chooses to use, and in the way it deploys them, relatively speaking the EU is capable of living up to both implications of Manners' 'normative power' terminology. If it is ratified, the Treaty of Lisbon may make this development clearer by strengthening the role of the High Representative and providing the Union with its own small External Action Service – but that, of course, remains to be seen.

THINK POINTS

- Why is the EU more powerful in some aspects of external policy than others?
- To what extent does the ESDP constitute a different approach to external policy from the EPC?
- How far can the EU rely on its economic power to achieve its objectives in global politics?
- Should the EU develop a more powerful and independent military capacity? Why?

FURTHER READING

Bretherton, Charlote and Vogler, John. (2006) *The European Union as a Global Actor* (2nd ed) (London: Routledge).
A useful guide to the EU's various roles on the world stage.

Hill, Christopher. and Smith, Michael E. (eds) (2005) *International Relations and the European Union* (Oxford: Oxford University Press).
This is an excellent collection of essays by leading authorities in the field, which sets out useful theoretical and empirical issues for the study of the EU's external policies.

Kagan, Robert (2004) *Paradise and Power: America and Europe in the New World Order* (London: Atlantic Books).
An eloquent sceptical view of the capacity of the Union to influence global politics.

Leonard, Mark (2005) *Why Europe Will Run the Twenty-First Century* (London: Fourth Estate).
An intriguing non-academic work which argues the EU is on the verge of becoming the most important global player.

Manners, Ian (2002) 'Normative Power Europe: A Contradiction in Terms?' *Journal of Common Market Studies* 40:2, 235–58.
This is the original article on normative power Europe.

CONTROVERSIES IN TODAY'S EUROPEAN UNION

INTRODUCTION

The purpose of this chapter is to explore some of the major problems and challenges on the European Union's (EU's) current agenda. Its aim is to give the reader a sound understanding of what these problems are, and why the EU continues to face serious difficulties despite almost sixty years of success. As a consequence, the chapter is not an examination of a range of policies in microscopic detail. Instead, it looks at the 'big picture': the EU system itself, and some of the most salient issues that the EU currently needs to address, such as democratic reform and future enlargements. It explains why certain important issues are particularly problematic for the Union and shows how issues of money and sovereignty explain the continued presence of these problems. In this way, the reader will be able to get to the heart of the EU's ongoing reform process, and develop an understanding of the principal challenges on the EU's current agenda.

Thus, after an initial explanatory section, the focus is on the difficulties and controversies of EU reform. Thereafter, a further section investigates the Treaty of Lisbon (ToL), and how it will change the EU system if it is ratified across the member states.

REFORMING THE EU: DIFFICULTIES
OF CHANGE

As the Union has evolved, and the integration of its member states has deepened, it has become more complex rather than simpler to understand. This complexity partly reflects, and partly causes, the Union's especially close acquaintance with controversy in recent years. It is necessary also to remember that crude power politics and member state intransigence can result in EU decisions that are either demonstrably unfair, such as the unequal treatment given to the 2004 entrant states with regard to regional policy money, or clearly unable to address the problems to hand, such as the indifferent Treaty of Nice.

Another key factor in explaining this continued controversy is the persistent diversity of member state ambitions for the EU. Certain member states continue to be generally favourable to the idea that the EU should become some form of federation, for example, Germany and Belgium. Others, such as the UK and the Czech Republic, continue to want the EU to be the tool of the member states, and very much subservient to them. This kind of continuing difference of opinion can also be found with regard to individual policies. Thus, one of the major contributing factors to the controversy of the EU reform process is the fact that there are so many different opinions about how any given issue should be addressed, and nobody is likely to be entirely happy with the compromise that is generated.

Sometimes, even when objectively workable solutions can be found, it is still impossible to reach agreement, and problems remain simply because no solution can be agreed: an example is the failure to agree on a common electoral system, and day for elections, to the European Parliament (EP). On other occasions, controversy persists because the member states have been able to agree reform, but in order to keep each other happy, and thus ensure they will all sign up to the eventual deal, they compromise so much that the solution which is eventually agreed is rather poor. A case in point is the 2003 reform to the Common Agricultural Policy (CAP), which, while making far greater progress towards liberalisation than many thought possible, remains inadequate in terms of environmental sustainability and correspondence with either the EU's own development policy objectives or the requirements of the World Trade Organisation (WTO).

Two other issues are also worth remembering when trying to explain the difficulties of EU reform. The first is perennial: the issue of national sovereignty.[1] The second is more telling now than at previous points in the EU's history: the issue of **juste retour** (fair return) on member state contributions to the EU budget. In the past, certain member states – notably the United Kingdom – have insisted that the EU must give them demonstrable financial benefits, so that they can justify the cost of membership to their publics. It was at least partly for this reason that the EU developed competence in regional policy. The need to demonstrate direct financial benefits from EU membership, other than those of the increased prosperity that has arisen from participation in the single market, now appears to be felt in increasing numbers of member states. Germany, for example, has made it clear that it is not happy to continue paying the lion's share of the EU budget, and that its post-reunification economic difficulties prohibit making increased contributions to the Union. Other 'net contributors' – those member states which pay more in to the EU budget than they receive directly from it – have voiced similar concerns. This was part of the reason why the Dutch voted against the Constitutional Treaty in 2005. In a time of increased euroscepticism (see below), and widespread economic difficulty, it is proving difficult for national governments to justify giving more money to the Union even if they wanted to. Many of them have no wish to even try. Thus, there is no, or little, money in the EU kitty for major new initiatives.[2]

The *juste retour* issue is an important point for more than financial reasons, however. This is because it implies that the EU is not to be supported out of idealism – i.e. the idea that integration is a good thing in and of itself – but rather out of calculations of supposed national self-interest. Thus, if the *juste retour* logic remains important, it can be expected that member states will wish to see a more direct relationship between what they want the EU to do, what they pay into the EU budget, and what the EU actually does. This would in all likelihood push the EU towards a more flexible system than it has currently developed. Such a development need not be negative (Warleigh 2002); however, it would certainly cause a break with orthodox approaches to the EU, particularly in the pro-European camp.

CONTROVERSIES IN EUROPEAN INTEGRATION: GOVERNANCE, ENLARGEMENT AND DEMOCRACY

Governance: some key challenges

Governance is concerned with how public policy decisions are made. As a concept, 'governance' implies a shift away from traditional forms of political structure, which had very clear and often hierarchical structures, towards systems where power is wielded in networks. As a practice, 'governance' implies a certain degree of messiness, by which I mean relatively unclear, or at least complex and overlapping structures, and decision-making via consensus-generation or partnership. It also implies that actors other than those traditionally associated with the use of power – elected politicians and civil servants – can be involved in decision-making about public policy issues. In recent times, most Western countries have experienced a shift towards governance and away from orthodox 'command-and-control' styles of politics: new levels of authority, especially global institutions such as the WTO, and different kinds of actor – especially businesses, but also citizens and civil society groups – have been granted a greater role in the making of public policy. Thus, governance brings both advantages and problems. It involves re-thinking the trade-off between transparency, or how easy it is to scrutinise what decision-makers do, and inclusion, or involving greater numbers of groups and actors. It also implies that new approaches to policy making will be necessary, i.e. that different methods must be used to address the perennial questions of politics: who gets what, how, when and why (Hudson and Lowe 2004).

BOX 6.1: KEY LEARNING POINT – GOVERNANCE, NOT GOVERNMENT, IN THE EU

In the specific case of the EU, the 'governance shift' is both a blessing and a problem. The Union's very creation could justifiably be seen as an early recognition of some of the pressures for the governance shift, because it involves the addition of a new mode of governance to its member states, not to mention the empowerment of the private sector via the single market and extensive opportunities to influence policy-making at the new level, and the generation of new ways of making policy. It has also often caused the creation of policy in what were, for many member states, hitherto virgin areas, such as environmental or competition policies. However, the EU also clearly demonstrates some of the dangers of the governance shift. This is largely because the decision-making systems that it uses are often opaque, and its reliance upon policy networks – sets of actors who co-operate to meet common objectives – is extensive. Transparency levels are therefore fairly low, and this in turn means that it can be difficult for the public to know who is really responsible for making EU policy decisions. As a result, accountability, the capacity to make those who wield public power answer for their decisions, is also low. Consequently, and with justification, there have been many allegations that the Union is undemocratic (see below) – although these claims can also be exaggerated.

In concrete terms, the principal challenge of EU governance is to re-design the way the Union works. The original system, set up in the 1950s, is no longer adequate to cope with either the massively expanded scope of the Union or the huge increase in the number of member states involved. Neither has the Union worked out a suitable accommodation between European and national levels of power – the subsidiarity and flexibility issues. Furthermore, the balance of power between the EU institutions themselves requires attention. Originally, the Monnet Method set out by the EU's founders favoured the Commission and Council over the EP. This balance has gradually and elliptically been re-visited in ad hoc ways, but there is now a clear need to acknowledge recent trends, especially the decline of the Commission and rise of the Parliament, and seek formally and openly to re-work the Monnet/Community Method.[3] Here, a key task will be to make the decision-making process more uniform and easier to understand.

A further task is to re-consider, or at least revise, the position of the European Court of Justice (ECJ). This Court, which has played such a crucial role in the integration process, is experiencing problems of two kinds. First, capacity issues arise because the ECJ's caseload is too heavy even after the establishment of the Court of First Instance (Hunt 2002). Second, political issues arise because the relationship between the ECJ/EC Law and national courts/law continues to be controversial. The most important example of this is the bitter dispute over '*Kompetenz-kompetenz*': the ability to deliver authoritative judgements about national sovereignty and the scope of EC law. Third, democracy issues arise because access to the ECJ for individuals rather than NGOs, member states or the EU institutions remains almost impossible.

The financial aspects of Union governance also require attention. Not only are there the budgetary issues mentioned above; there are in addition issues of how the Union's budget is spent, with allegations of fraud surfacing occasionally. This became the hottest of issues in 1999, and led to the resignation of the Commission in order to avoid being sacked by the EP; since then, efforts have been made to improve the situation, but the Court of Auditors still regularly refuses to sign off on the EU's accounts. It would not be fair to blame the EU institutions entirely for this problem: they have improved their procedures significantly in recent years. Moreover, it is often outside agents and national officials who are responsible for programme delivery and proper production of the relevant paperwork. Nonetheless, this is a problem for the EU in terms of public relations, especially in countries which are net donors to the EU budget.

Policy implementation is a further problem for the Union. Although member states are in principle subject to fines for non-compliance with EU policy, and the supremacy of EU law over national law with which it conflicts has long been established, there are far too many cases of national failure to implement Union legislation which escape punishment, either because the Commission is unaware of them or because it chooses not to take action for political reasons. This is even true in high profile cases, such as the blatant disregard of the Stability and Growth Pact in recent years by France and Germany. Given the recent trend towards soft policy, indeed, member states' capacity to fail to implement EU policies has indubitably been increased, since there are few mechanisms for policing this in such forms of policy-making. Of course, member states *may* be shamed into complying by such means as 'scoreboards', and can even be persuaded to do so as part of broader package deals on a range of policies. Nonetheless, where there are no ultimate means of discovering non-compliance or ensuring member states step up to the mark, implementation of policies at national level may well be patchy. In order to combat this, it may be necessary to give the Union further teams of inspectors with the ability to seek out cases of non-compliance, following the model of competition policy, where such inspectors play a vital role.

The final key challenge of governance in the present day Union is to revise certain policies in order to make them more effective. Examples here include further change to the CAP in order to make it more environmentally sustainable, to the Stability and Growth Pact in order to allow governments in the euro-zone to take more effective interventionist steps when their economies are experiencing 'negative growth', and reform of the EU's foreign and security policies so that the Union is capable of defining and pursuing its objectives in these fields effectively.

Managing enlargement

On the face of it, EU enlargement appears to place the burden of change on applicant states rather than current members or the EU system itself. After all, it is the new members which have to adopt the entire EU *acquis*, and for them to adapt their systems to fit the Union, not the other way round. Moreover, the Union has enlarged six times already, and has plenty of experience in managing the process. However, such assumptions are inaccurate for two major reasons. First, the 2004–7 enlargement rounds were of an unprecedented scale: between 1973 and 1995, the EU admitted nine new member states, all from Western Europe, and in 2004–7 it took in 12 more, at least 10 of which have very different histories and perspectives from the previous members as they are former Communist states. Second, the 2004 and 2007 enlargements are of an unprecedented nature: the new member states range from the micro-state of Malta to the politically and geographically large state of Poland, and the average wealth of the new states is far below that of even the poorest pre-existing member state.

Thus, the process of enlargement to the countries of Central and Eastern Europe, Malta and Cyprus throws up many challenges to the EU. Some of these are institutional, and may be complex, but are essentially issues of adjusting the current system and budget. An example is agreeing the voting weights of the new member states in the Council, and the number of MEPs they should each have.

Other issues are cultural – for example, socialising citizens of the 2004 entrant states into the EU system and way of doing politics, so that they can play their proper part in the Union. Since 2004, there have been signs that in at least some of the new member states, liberal political values are not very well entrenched: for example, Poland has acquired a reputation for boorish and reactionary social values. Further issues are managerial and resource-related. An example is finding the money and skills to provide Union legislation in the official languages of the new member states, as well as interpreters able to translate from, say, Finnish to French and then Bulgarian, so that politicians and members of the public from the new member states can take part in the policy process effectively and on an equal basis. Most of these issues are capable of resolution with sufficient forethought and money.

However, there are other major issues brought centre-stage by enlargement that are harder to address. These are fundamental to the nature of the EU. First, the 2007 enlargement made it much more overt that some members of the EU club are more equal than others, and that new member states can be placed under special obligations to improve their political and legal systems even after joining. Thus, Romania and Bulgaria are due to be monitored in their fight against corruption and judicial reform process to ensure they make a successful transition to liberal democracy. Although it could be argued that this simply makes overt occasional practice in the past, for example Greek accession to the Union, the fact that this monitoring is official marks a clear departure from previous enlargements, when all applicant countries had to be *declared* ready before they joined. The implications of this for future enlargements, particularly the possible entry of Turkey or Serbia, are extremely interesting.

A second such fundamental issue is the need for the EU-15 – those states that had joined the Union before 2004 – to accept the sacrifice of a certain degree of power and money if the more recent entrants are to become full members of the Union in reality as well as in law. Some of the bargains that have been made to ensure the EU is able to make policy in certain areas are simply unsustainable after the 2004 enlargement, and the reform of the budget remains controversial: as I write, a review of the 'financial perspective' for after 2014 is yet to be completed, and it will be a crucial test of whether the big issues in budgetary reform such as agricultural subsidies or the various rebates such as that given to the UK are capable of resolution. Since 2004, it has become evident that new coalitions between states are necessary to gain support in the Council, so that traditional power relationships may be thrown over to some extent. That said, it does still appear that the Franco-German axis can play a vital role in the process of decision-making at the very top level, as shown by the partnership between Angela Merkel and Nicolas Sarkozy in brokering the Lisbon Treaty. Furthermore, the 2004 and 2007 enlargements have forced several issues up the EU agenda might otherwise have suffered benign neglect. These issues include security and economic relations with Russia, especially after Moscow's alleged cyber-war on the Baltic states and the EU–Russia 'meat war' over Polish pork. However, they also cover Turkey's application to join the Union, which is arguably made more complex and more salient after Cypriot entry, and relations with the USA, whose military superiority and market-size inferiority are made even clearer by the recent expansions of the Union. Thus, managing the latest round of enlargement will require the EU to commit further resources, and to re-think both some of its existing policies and many of its strategic priorities. This will include its attitude towards, and capacity for, future enlargements: it appears that Serbia may be fast-tracked to membership in order to help resolve the issue of Kosovo's independence, and yet for some unfathomable reason talk of the so-called enlargement fatigue is bandied about when the conversation switches to Turkey.

Democracy

Tackling the 'democratic deficit' is a major challenge facing the Union. Some of the issues that must be addressed as part of any solution are systemic, and some relate to issues of managing increased diversity with fairness and equality. Both these sets of issues have been discussed immediately above. However, there are further issues which require urgent attention rather than the fanciful rhetoric which has generally been their lot so far. Questions such as *fair representation* (citizens must know that insofar as representative democracy is considered important in a transnational system, their representatives are accountable and have a transparent and useful function), *access to justice* (citizens must be able to use the ECJ in order to gain redress from governments, EU institutions, companies or individuals whose transgression of EC law causes them injury), and *participation* (citizens must both want, and be able, to take part in the EU decision-making process) are of the utmost and immediate importance. This is because much of the general public 'euroscepticism' is well-founded. The EU does not operate as a democracy, and, although it is far less anti-democratic than any other international or transnational organisation, this situation is untenable (Warleigh 2003). In particular, and as a first step, the Union needs to encourage its citizens to engage with both itself and each other. This is so that citizens can both shape the Union more clearly according to their priorities, and thus potentially begin to consider it more legitimate. It should also help them to develop the habit of working with citizens from other member states in order to meet their shared goals, thereby adding a 'European' element to their own political identities. However, after the failed referenda on the Constitutional Treaty in both the Netherlands and France, EU elites may be reluctant to take bold action in this direction: when you ask the people what they want, they may not say what you want to hear!

TACKLING THE ISSUES? TREATY CHANGE SINCE NICE

The Convention on the future of Europe and the Draft Constitution of 2003

In fairness to both the Union and its member states, it must be stated that attempts to deal with many, if not all, of these issues have been frequent in recent years, although institutional change has often been more apparent than reform of the most problematic policies, such as the CAP. Since the Maastricht Treaty, there have been two successfully ratified further Treaties (Amsterdam and Nice), a complex process of agreeing a Constitutional Treaty and its revision after member states rejected the first draft, and more recently the ToL, elaborated after the second version of the Constitutional Treaty failed to survive referenda in France and the Netherlands. Thus, the Union has amassed a great deal of experience in matters of constitutional reform, and a track record of doing so on an almost constant basis.

One of the most interesting aspects of this ongoing reform agenda has been the willingness of the member states to experiment with unusual methods of drafting Treaties. Typically, international organisations produce such change, if they do so at all, via a process of diplomatic bargaining. In the EU, this process is known as an IGC, or intergovernmental conference, and it brings together the heads of state and government from all the member states, as well as non-voting representatives of the Commission and EP, to thrash out a new deal. However, it became clear throughout the 1990s that this method of working was no longer very successful. The Treaty of Amsterdam was far less ambitious than that of Maastricht, and failed in its specific task of dealing with the 'left-overs' from that Treaty. The Treaty of Nice was even less successful, failing to address many of the most important issues of the day and once again leaving unresolved certain matters which had remained on the table since Maastricht (Neunreither 2000). Thus, although it is true that the Amsterdam and Nice Treaties made a greater impact on the Union than is often acknowledged (Church and Phinnemore 2002), they were scarcely the great steps forward that were required to address the problems identified above. Moreover, especially at Nice, the problems of the IGC method became apparent when inept chairing by the French Presidency worsened the already high tensions in and between national capitals, and almost brought the EU to a standstill.

Thus, after Nice, even the European Council agreed that a new way of addressing the issues of Union reform had to be found if progress was to be made. The method that was chosen drew on recent Union experience with the drafting of the Charter of Fundamental Rights, which had been developed by a Convention composed of national and EU-level members. This Convention proved that public, long-term deliberation could be more effective than behind-closed-doors diplomacy in reaching a generally acceptable policy outcome. As a result, the European Council agreed at Laeken in 2001 to establish a Convention on the Future of Europe, whose duty would be to deliberate upon certain key issues and produce an agreement which could then form the basis of discussions in another, hopefully shorter and less acrimonious, IGC. Thus, the role of the IGC remained crucial – it would be the body with the ultimate power of decision – but it was expected that at the very least the Convention would be a means whereby agreement could be forged on controversial issues, and that as they were participants in those deliberations the member governments would more-or-less stick by the Convention's decisions (Magnette 2002).

The Convention was composed of representatives of the national governments of the member states, the national parliaments of the member states, the EP and the European Commission. The states scheduled for membership of the Union in 2004 also sent representatives of their respective governments and parliaments. Led by Valéry Giscard d'Estaing, a former President of France, and his two Vice-Presidents Jean-Luc Dehaene (former Prime Minister of Belgium) and Giuliano Amato (former Italian Foreign Minister) the Convention had a high profile and involved important 'heavyweight' politicians. It was clearly established as a body that could expect to be influential, drawing on experts from both national and EU levels, and involving the member governments at every stage so that their acquiescence in whatever the Convention ultimately produced could in principle be taken as likely. This status continued throughout the Convention's life, as testified by the late membership of extremely important politicians such as the German Foreign Minister, Joschka Fischer, when national representatives stood down and had to be replaced.

The Convention worked by deliberation, i.e. by an attempt to find a consensus view based on genuine accommodation of the various members' differences, rather than by the IGC methods (generating package deals and power games where vetoes are threatened in order to force concessions). Its deliberations lasted a year, and eventually a Draft Constitution for the EU was produced. This document took 'decisive steps' towards a Union based on the principles of representative government and the rule of law (Pinder 2003). As such, it strengthened the formal elements of federalism in the EU (Federal Union 2003), but it did not find answers to all of the most important problems of the Union's structure and institutions. It neglected, for example, to make recommendations on matters such as reform of the Court of Justice, or to reform of the Stability and Growth Pact and/or the mandate of the European Central Bank in order to allow a more Keynesian approach to monetary policy. However, the DC made genuine and useful progress on a range of issues that had become increasingly salient in EU governance. These ranged from matters of institutional roles and powers to making the Union more 'user-friendly' in terms of reduced complexity and increasing the formal aspects of its legitimacy. Consequently, the Draft Constitution was a major step forward in the Union's reform process.

However, it proved to be too big a step for some of the heads of state/government to accept, even though their representatives on the Convention had all approved it. At the European Council meeting of December 2003, disagreement over the definition of a 'qualified majority' in voting in the Council of Ministers derailed the Draft Constitution, because some of the member states that felt they would lose power under the new definition – Poland and Spain – refused to agree to the Convention's proposal. The other member states insisted that it was both necessary and acceptable; amid high drama, the summit meeting collapsed without a deal, and the Draft Constitution as such came to nothing. At that time, it appeared that the Convention had thus been something of a failed experiment.

From the Constitutional Treaty to the Treaty of Lisbon

As a result, the Irish Presidency of the EU in 2004 inherited a very difficult situation; if a new Treaty was to be agreed, this extremely difficult issue of voting rights would have to be addressed. Finding a solution would require very high calibre diplomacy, and also the capacity to walk the line between offering new compromises in order to persuade Spain and Poland to sign up without alienating the member states which had already agreed, or sending the signal that member states who used brinkmanship would always do better than those who played the game with more solidarity. In the event, the Irish achieved a deal much more quickly than had been anticipated, and by the end of 2004 established a new Constitutional Treaty, which carried over much of the text of the Draft Constitution, but which also secured a new agreement on the definition of a qualified majority. Thus, a great part of the Convention's deliberations were included in the new Constitutional Treaty, which was put out to rati- fication in the member states.

As has been stated several times above, this new version of the Treaty was then shot down by the citizens of France and the Netherlands in 2005, and as new Treaties must be agreed in each member state, the Constitutional Treaty as such died. This provoked a profound shock in Brussels and in many national capitals, and

plunged the Union into an existential crisis. Policy-making continued, and the euro continued to function; but the system itself
remained as established at Nice in 2000, and a sense of direction was
notably lacking. In addition, questions of the EU's legitimacy
abounded; had the integration process itself, rather than the
Constitutional Treaty, been rejected in two of the original member
states? If there had been a referendum in other states after France
and the Netherlands – they were scheduled subsequently to take
place in Ireland and also in the UK – would these plebiscites have
produced rejections of the new Treaty too?

The official response to the rejection of the Constitutional Treaty
was to call a Period of Reflection, and to engage in discussion with
so-called stakeholders, including civil society organisations, about
how to find a way forward. It also resulted in a bid to establish exactly
why the Treaty had been rejected in the two states, and whether there
could be ways of refining it in order to make it acceptable there, while
preserving its popularity in the states which had already ratified it
before the votes in France and the Netherlands. Eventually, in a re-
run of the Irish diplomatic coup of 2004, the German Presidency of
the Council brokered the contents of a new deal in 2007, and this
resulted in the signing of the ToL in December of that year. It is on
this Treaty that reform efforts currently depend.

THE TREATY OF LISBON: WHAT DIFFERENCE
WOULD IT MAKE?

There are several significant measures in the ToL, although some of
them, such as the new rules on majority voting and the changes to
the number of Commissioners, will not enter into force immediately
on ratification as a result of pressure from certain member states.[4]
Taken together, they could, if the ToL is ratified, go some way to
resolving several of the Union's key institutional problems. As its
focus is on institutions and processes, the Treaty does not in itself
include proposals for radical change to the EU's major policies.
However, by clarifying the qualified majority rule, and simplifying it;
by extending the powers of the EP, including, for the first time, into
legislation on agricultural policy; by providing the EU with a more
stable leadership (the Presidency of the European Council would be
elected for two and a half years, rather than 'rotated' between the

member states every six months); and by extending the capacity of the Union to run its foreign policy operations (by establishing a European External Action Service, effectively an EU diplomatic corps), the new Treaty would arguably make it easier to make these changes in the future.

In terms of the main political institutions of the Union, the principal changes that would be introduced are as follows.

The *European Council* was made a full EU institution, which entrenches it at the heart of the EU system. The European Council was given a permanent Presidency (to be elected every two and a half years), removing the previous arrangement whereby the Presidency rotates between the member states every six months. The President of the European Council would be tasked with running the institution, but also with representing the EU externally in matters of the

---

BOX 6.2: KEY LEARNING POINT – PRINCIPAL CHANGES IN THE TREATY OF LISBON

- The EU was given its own legal personality.
- The Union's decision-making procedures were simplified (with co-decision and qualified majority voting in Council becoming the standard procedure).
- The Union's structures were simplified, and the 'third pillar' (police and judicial co-operation in criminal matters) was abolished.
- The division of responsibilities between the EU and the member states was further clarified.
- The Charter of Fundamental Rights was made legally binding, although not part of the ToL itself.
- The rules for qualified majority voting were simplified, and the extremely complicated formula for 'weighting' the votes of the various member states was abolished. Instead, a 'qualified majority' would consist of 55% of the member states, if they represented 65% of the EU population.
- The competence of the EU in matters of justice and home affairs was increased by the abolition of Pillar III and the transfer of competence in these areas to pillar.

- The role of national parliaments in EU decision-making was increased; national parliaments were given the power to act as the Union's 'subsidiarity watchdog', and the right to block EU legislation, in partnership with a majority in either Council or the EP.
- The EU's external policy was made more coherent, with the confirmation of the High Representative of the EU for the CFSP, and by making this official a Vice President of the Commission, with her/his own secretariat, the External Action Service.
- The creation of a Citizens' Initiative right, whereby EU citizens can request the Commission to produce legislation on particular issues that they consider important.
- The provision for states to secede from the Union.

Source: Europolitics 2007.

common foreign and security policy. This means that external representation of the Union may be facilitated; it will remain complex, however – see below.

The *Council of the EU* (Council of Ministers) is also reformed by the ToL. The General Affairs Council was given a new role as the means of coordinating work between the Council of Ministers and the European Council, and was also transformed into a public legislature – a major step forward in terms of transparency and accountability. The High Representative for CFSP would chair the Foreign Affairs Council, and, together with helping make the EU's common foreign and security policy, he or she would be responsible for its running.

The *European Commission* is reduced in size by the ToL, or at least there will be fewer Commissioners in the College. Instead of one Commissioner from each member state, as at present, if the ToL is ratified there will be a number of Commissioners that is equivalent to two-thirds of the number of member states, with those states which do not have a Commissioner in one College guaranteed one in the next. So, in an EU of 27, there would be 18 Commissioners, and if Finland had one in 2014–2019, it might not in 2019–2024, but if Denmark had not had one in 2014–2019, it would be guaranteed one in 2019–2024. This should make the College more effective and ensure it can concentrate on key policy portfolios. The *President of the Commission* would be elected by the EP: the sole candidate for the post would be nominated by the European Council, but before nomination the Council would have to consult the EP, and wait for the result of EP elections, to ensure that the nominated candidate would be likely to gain majority support in the EP. The remaining Commissioners will still require approval from the EP before they take up their posts, although they will still be nominated by the member states, and selected on that basis by the Commission President before presentation to the EP.

The *European Parliament* is given greater legislative powers, as co-decision is standardised as the 'ordinary legislative procedure'. This involves an extension of co-decision to several issue areas, but two are particularly of note: the EU's budget, where the EP's powers had previously been limited to non-compulsory expenditure, i.e. the smaller part of the budget, and to the CAP. The EP is also given new competences in the area of justice and home affairs, because Pillar III is abolished, and once-intergovernmental matters will thus become subject to the ordinary legislative procedure. The EP's existing powers to hold the Commission to account were confirmed, and its role in the election of the Commission President is strengthened.

In addition to these reforms, the ToL also includes several other measures of significance. The rights of the member states, and also national parliaments, are increased in the ToL. Enhanced cooperation, and an equivalent in foreign policy, permanent structured cooperation, are both facilitated, which may make it easier for the EU to make progress in certain areas of policy where several, but not all, member states want to deepen their cooperation, while respecting the rights of those states which choose not to take part. In what may prove to be the most important institutional innovation of the Treaty, national parliaments are given the right to act as the Union's 'subsidiarity watchdog'. If 50% of national parliaments object to a proposal from the Commission, they can force the withdrawal of the proposal if they can secure the support of either 55% of the member states in Council or an absolute majority of MEPs. This should promote a stronger engagement of national parliaments in the EU decision-making process, deepening links between themselves and also with

EU-level institutions. It would add a novel dimension to the Union's legislative process, and make that process much more clearly multi-level in nature.

The ToL confirms the post of the High Representative for CFSP, but makes that post more authoritative by joining its functions in the Council to a key job in the Commission; if the ToL is ratified, the High Representative will become the Commission's Vice President, and the role of External Policy Commissioner will be abolished as a result. The High Representative is also given his/her own diplomatic corps, the External Action Service.

The structure and rules for future rule change of the Union are both simplified by the ToL. Pillar III is abolished, and its tasks are taken into Pillar I; Pillar II remains, but the differences between Pillars I and II would be reduced given the increasing overlap between matters of domestic policy and those of security – is the issue of the exchange of citizens' personal data between the EU and the USA, for example, entirely a matter of migration policy, or does it have security policy, as well as civil liberties, aspects too? Future Treaty change would be possible by a unanimous vote in the European Council, but this could not be used to add to the EU's competences, only to change the existing system.

The symbolic aspects of the ToL are very interesting. On one hand, the elements of the Constitutional Treaty that many Eurosceptics objected to, considering them to confer effective statehood on the Union, are gone: there is now to be no official EU flag or hymn, and May 9th will not be an official EU-wide public holiday. This is clearly a battle lost by the federalists, even if the flag and hymn remain at the unofficial level. On the other hand, the ToL explicitly gives the Union more powers in environmental issues – especially the fight against climate change – and social policy (Avery *et al.* 2007), thereby stressing the need for common action and solidarity in the face of major problems. The role of the free market economy is also made less central as an *objective* of the Union, allowing the ToL to be presented in a more social democratic light than the Constitutional Treaty, although the *acquis* regarding the single market and euro is not substantially altered. However, the Charter of Fundamental Rights is not included in the ToL. Instead, there is a new Protocol attached to the Treaty, which states that the Charter will have the same legal status as if it were part of the Treaty!

There are no radical changes to the ECJ, or to the ECB and the **EMU** regime. However, the Euro-zone will gain the power to have external representation in international financial organisations. This makes sense in terms of maximising the voice of the euro-zone states, but it will add to the complexity of the EU's external representation.

CONCLUSIONS: CAN THE LISBON TREATY SOLVE THE EU'S PROBLEMS?

An initial, but obvious, comment to make here is that if it is not ratified in each of the member states the ToL will make no difference whatsoever. Given the fate of the Constitutional Treaty, it is not safe simply to assume that such ratification will be smooth; only Ireland will hold a referendum, but even if the Irish vote in favour, it must be possible, if unlikely, that a national parliament somewhere might block it.

A second issue to consider is whether the ToL is really very different from the Constitutional Treaty. This matters because if the two are largely the same, it might be claimed that the EU elites (for which read the member state governments) are trying to revive much of the text that citizens thought had been killed off. Certainly, opponents of the Treaty have argued that this is the case: the think-tank Open Europe has stated that the two Treaties are 96% the same (Open Europe 2007: 4). Although how this figure is derived must be open to question, it must be acknowledged that the two texts *are* essentially similar. The key points of the deal summed up in the ToL were already established by the Convention, and there was no real desire at the EU level to unpick that bargain. Instead, attention was paid to resolving the objections of those states who returned to the Qualified Majority Voting (QMV) issue, using the collapse of the Constitutional Treaty as an opportunity to reopen this debate, and on providing what are intended to be the means of assuaging public concerns in the Netherlands and France. Those member states which presented 'red lines' to their peers – issues on which they would refuse to compromise, such as the UK and Ireland's insistence that tax policy remain at national level – had them respected. Thus, no major new bargains were made as part of a new package deal.

However, there are some important differences between the ToL and the Constitutional Treaty. First, the symbolic elements of the

Constitutional Treaty and its predecessor have been removed, signal-
ling the non-statehood of the Union. Second, the provisions on QMV
are tougher, albeit only slightly. Third, the 'subsidiarity watchdog'
role of national parliaments is improved: the Constitutional Treaty
gave a third of national parliaments the right to raise an objection to
a new EU proposal, but no means to enforce their objections; the ToL
raises the bar to half of the national parliaments, but gives them the
ability to block the proposal entirely in alliance with either the
Council or the EP. This is a sophisticated reading of the EU's multi-
level needs for legitimacy and would in all likelihood increase the
mutual understanding of national parliaments across the Union,
as well as that between the national and European tiers of parlia-
mentarians. Less helpfully, however, the ToL reverts to the classic
form of EU treaties, i.e. it is an addition to the existing documents
rather than the replacement of them with a single new text, which
the Constitutional Treaty had aimed to be. Thus, the actual texts of
the Union treaties will be more complex, and more prolix, than in the
past – which will not help the Union's transparency.

Will the ToL improve the Union's legitimacy? The likely answer
to this question is yes-and-no. On the positive side, agreeing and
implementing the new Treaty would improve the credibility of the
EU, and demonstrate it can still deal with major issues of Treaty
change. This is likely to reduce some of the scepticism about the
Union. It also contains several measures which could improve the
Union's working democracy, especially regarding the new role for
national parliaments. On the negative side, the ToL results from a
classic piece of EU elite politics, and the decision not to subject it to
referenda except where the national constitution made this ineluc-
ble reinforces the message that the EU is out of touch with the citizen. It will be important for the new measures included in the ToL to
improve the balance between elites and citizens to be implemented
quickly, and to be supplemented with other measures too, if this
impression is to be countered.

There remain some fairly large 'left-overs'. The organisational
problems and capacity of the ECJ have not been adequately addressed,
and, from a social democratic point of view, the lack of change to
the single currency regime is problematic. Enhanced cooperation
is facilitated, and this may make progress on some areas of policy
that cannot successfully be addressed by the EU as a whole easier;

however, this is by no means certain, and the normative role of flexibility remains to be clarified. The external representation of the Union has arguably been made more complex: the fact that the new European Council President, High Representative, and Euro-zone representative will all have responsibilities here opens up potential for some intriguing turf battles.

In sum, however, the ToL is a useful step forward. Its genesis is rather unfortunate, and it is not as simple a text as the original Draft Constitution, or even the Constitutional Treaty. It does not contain answers to all the Union's major problems. However, it does make more progress on these than the Amsterdam and Nice Treaties, and as a result it should help the EU function effectively, while generating the basis for further action to be taken in future on a policy by policy basis, if there is the political will. That is, if it is ratified …

THINK POINTS

- Why has it proved very difficult for intergovernmental conferences to solve the EU's major problems?
- On balance, were the 2004 and 2007 enlargement processes beneficial for both the EU-15 and the new member states? Why (not)?
- Do you think the Convention on the Future of Europe was a successful experiment? Should any future EU Treaties be prepared in a similar way? If not, which alternatives would you suggest?
- How significant are the differences between the Constitutional Treaty and the ToL?

FURTHER READING

Church, Clive and Phinnemore, David (2002) *The Penguin Guide to the European Treaties* (London: Penguin).
An impressive guide to the history and process of making Treaties in the EU, which also includes the key Treaties themselves.

Magnette, Paul (2005) *What is the European Union? Nature and Prospects* (Basingstoke: Palgrave).
A first-rate analysis of the EU and how its unusual nature affects its evolution.

If you want to keep up-to-date with the EU and its Treaty change process, as well as policy reform, there are many websites to consult (see Appendix I). The principal academic journals in the area are *JCMS: Journal of Common Market Studies*, the *Journal of European Public Policy*, *Comparative European Politics*, the *Journal of European Integration*, the increasingly incongruously-named *West European Politics*, and *European Union Politics*. The JCMS also publishes the *JCMS Annual Review*, which retrospectively evaluates the principal developments in the Union every year.

The most useful daily newspaper on EU issues in English is the *Financial Times*.

An interesting weekly newspaper which details all the events in the 'Brussels village' – that is, the EU policy-making world – is *European Voice*.

WHERE NOW FOR THE
EUROPEAN UNION?

INTRODUCTION: DIFFERENT PERSPECTIVES
ON THE SAME QUESTION

Thinking about the future of the European Union (EU) is complicated for many reasons. First, unanticipated events could occur, and
have a tremendous impact on what the EU does, and how it does it.
A case in point is the fall of Communism in Central and Eastern
Europe. Second, no matter how entrenched a particular government
or member state is in its advocacy of, or opposition to, a given issue,
these preferences can change. A government could lose a national
election and be replaced by another with different policies. Calculations
of national interest can alter. A good example is UK opposition to EU
social policy, which was revised, but not wholly abandoned, upon the
arrival in power of the Labour Party in 1997. Third, in the process of
bargaining and deal-making that produces both policy decisions on
'everyday' matters and the grand decisions about EU reform, complex trading can result in unanticipated outcomes. Fourth, EU institutions can have a significant impact on the Union in a way that
neither the member governments, nor arguably the institutions
themselves, entirely anticipated. An illustration is the impact of
the European Court of Justice in determining the legal order of the
EU through its decisions in cases like *Van Gend*.[1] Fifth, domestic

institutions and events can have a role in shaping the development of the Union: for example, referenda can change the content of EU treaties, at least as they apply to a particular member state, and even derail them entirely, as happened after the referenda on the Constitutional Treaty in France and the Netherlands. Additionally, national courts can and do play a key function in developing the Union legal order.

However, perhaps the key difficulty in trying to think about the EU's future evolution is the issue of the suitable conceptual lens. Different theories of European integration have generated widely disparate understandings of the EU's possible futures from roughly the same data: metaphorically speaking, the same glass can be seen to be both half-full *and* half-empty. Depending on which theory – or 'lens' – is used to study the Union, different interpretations of how the EU works, what its possible futures are, and how it is present should be interpreted, are generated. Until the 1990s, most scholars of the EU simply used intergovernmentalist or neofunctionalist lenses, developing rival accounts of the integration process. More recently, attempts have been made to develop a theory of European integration by joining together the key insights developed by **intergovernmentalism** and **neofunctionalism** in a kind of mega-theory. However, these attempts proved largely unsuccessful (Warleigh 1998), and as a result most scholars interested in EU theory have gone back to basics and devoted themselves to understanding particular aspects of the EU system, institutions or policies, or on the Europeanisation effect of integration on national policies and systems (see Chapter 2).

As a result, most scholars agree that the present day Union can best be understood as a system of 'multi-level governance', a partially autonomous system with deep roots in, and dependence on, its member states, but also with significant capacity to exert independent influence on policy (Hooghe and Marks 2001; Bache and Flinders 2004). No other international organisation has the same breadth and depth of powers; no other international organisation has a directly elected Parliament or quasi-Supreme Court; no international organisation has its own currency; and yet, given its lack of a standing army, limited competence in foreign policy, comparatively tiny budget and lack of taxation power, the EU falls far short of what we would expect of a (federal) state too. Thus, although there are many gains to be had from studying the EU in comparison with global governance institutions and other regional organisations such as ASEAN or **NAFTA** (Warleigh-Lack 2007), scholars have often shied away from positing models of its future development, perhaps cowed by the weaknesses of previous attempts to generate such theory.

However, in some parts of EU studies, enormous attention has been paid to these issues. The literature on EU democracy and legitimacy is replete with analyses of the EU system and suggestions of ways in which it might be reformed (for an overview, see Warleigh 2003). The literature on the EU's external policy is often linked to theoretically-driven analyses of its essence and possible development (Kagan 2004; Leonard 2005; Zielonka 2006). Policy-makers and even citizens have devoted attention to this issue throughout the decade, initially prompted by the Commission's need to reform itself and re-claim centrality in the institutional constellation, which produced the White Paper on European Governance in 2001, but more recently in the context of the attempts to produce the Constitutional Treaty – and to manage its rejection. As a result, it is a fitting way to bring the book to a close.

The structure of the chapter is as follows. First, I set out several possible scenarios for the future of the Union, and, where appropriate, point out their links with particular theories of either European integration or international politics. These scenarios are not intended as predictions. Nor are they all-encompassing. Rather, they are intended to serve as illustrations of some of the possible futures for the EU, and are written as retrospectives from the perspective of an imaginary future narrator attempting to explain how the various scenarios had arisen. Second, I discuss the factors which appear most likely, at the time of writing, to have a significant impact on the development of the EU in the short to immediate term. Finally, I argue that current evidence points towards a future that bears a remarkably close resemblance to the present, albeit one in which both the complexity and flexibility of the Union are increased.

EUROPE 2025: THREE POSSIBLE FUTURES

The European Federation

After the Lisbon Treaty was ratified, European elites breathed a sigh of relief. Almost a whole decade spent trying to move on from the

Nice Treaty had finally been concluded; the EU could now focus on using its reasonably streamlined system to make progress on some of the big issues of the day. The arrangements to extend QMV and the 'double majority' principle went down well; it was easier for citizens to understand than previous arrangements, and although it could not in itself remove the Union's legitimacy problems it did go some way towards making Union policy-making more transparent – particularly when the EP and Council came to an informal agreement to publish on their respective websites the minutes from conciliation meetings.

The External Action Service (EAS) was duly set up, and over the years between 2009 and 2014 they established solid relationships with key actors in Brussels and also in national capitals. Ever wary of the need to balance the often opposing interests of the Union's two biggest military players – 'Europeanist' France and 'Atlanticist' Britain – the EAS garnered a reputation for competence and helpfulness that soon won it plaudits in London and Paris. Perhaps more grudgingly, there was also support in Washington, which admired the manner in which Serbia and the remaining Balkan states had either joined, or were on the verge of joining, the Union and thus become enmeshed in the continental governance and security system. Of course, it was necessary to play a difficult balancing game between the High Representative for Foreign Policy, who was increasingly the focal point for third countries seeking contact with the EU, and the Presidents of both the Commission and the European Council, who could make rival and equally valid claims to leadership. However, as President of the European Council between 2009 and 2014, Mary Robinson proved a versatile diplomat, using the fact she came from neutral Ireland to great effect in avoiding public tensions with the High Representative; continuing in office as Commission President for the same period, José Manuel Barroso was content to focus on economic reform and planning the realisation of a deeper economic governance regime for the Union, or at least the euro-zone, backed by France's President Sarkozy.

Thus, by 2014, all appeared to be rosy in the EU garden. Potential institutional clashes were avoided, and the effectively bicameral legislative system between the Council and EP even managed, somewhat belatedly, to make citizens more willing to engage with the EU system – particularly after the election of the passionate and engaging Green MEP Daniel Cohn-Bendit to the Presidency of the

Parliament after a funding scandal brought low all the principal candidates from the centre-left and centre-right. The euro continued to function well, and as more and more member states joined it upon meeting the entry criteria, it was increasingly becoming the world's reserve currency. The only institutional change since Lisbon had been to extend the term in office of the European Council President to a renewable term of five years, which was generally viewed as a sensible tie-in with the cycles of both the Commission and the EP, and had been agreed using the simplified revision procedure rather than an IGC.

However, below the surface were problems waiting to wreak havoc like so many malignant cancers. The EU system was working fairly effectively, but it was not always doing what most citizens wanted it to do. Thus, the Union still had a legitimacy problem, which was particularly acute given that the member states still kept the Union's budget relatively small, and thereby ensured it could not, with its own resources, tackle issues of wealth redistribution or cross-border solidarity in any great depth. By 2018, a crisis point was reached thanks to climate change, whose effects had been becoming more and more obvious in the preceding years. As huge coastal stretches of several member states became submerged under water, and as increasing numbers of refugees entered the Union from Africa and the Middle East, citizens began to demand more from the EU since it was clear that national governments could not address the issues effectively on their own. In Spain, for example, it simply was not possible to cope with the thousands of refugees from West Africa – particularly as the desertification of Spain itself, not to mention large stretches of the member states around the Adriatic and Mediterranean, was causing massive problems of social dislocation and disrupting the agricultural cycle. And yet, the EU could not act effectively, since it had neither the human resources nor the cash.

Making matters worse was the fact that these problems were due to climate change, an issue that Russia and the USA still failed to take seriously despite the fact it was as harmful there as anywhere else. In the USA, the grip of the oil industry over campaign finance was just proving too hard a nut to crack, and Washington had in 2010 ensured the so-called Bali roadmap on climate change policy of the UN actually led nowhere; in Russia, President-for-life Vladimir Putin continued to focus on the use of energy supply as a key foreign policy tool

WHERE NOW FOR THE EUROPEAN UNION? 119

and revenue-generator, and thus Russia was by no means inclined to acknowledge that fossil fuels such as those it was exporting in huge quantities could make a significant contribution to climate change. Outside the EU, only China, determined to become a full superpower, had realised that greening its development plans would not only bring kudos at the UN and with the EU, helping its 'peaceful rise', but it would also consolidate its position as a market leader in green energy and technology, in which it envisaged massive future profits. This policy also made Beijing usefully independent of both the Arab states and Moscow. Thus, neither the EU's closest Western ally, nor its nearest large neighbour, were likely sources of support in finding real solutions to the EU's problems, although both President Jed Bush of the USA and President Putin sent messages of support. China was quietly pleased to see its only major rival in the green technology businesses suffer such difficulties, and offered rather limited help in the form of market access rights that the Union was in no position to take up.

The crunch came when 40 million signatures were placed on a Citizens' Initiative petition, calling on the Commission to draft a Constitution for Europe. It was accompanied by similar, if smaller, petitions in each member state, whether with legal status or not. The Commission, now headed by Meglena Kuneva, wisely passed the buck to President Angela Merkel, who had left German politics to become President of the European Council after Mary Robinson. She undertook a frantic round of diplomacy, much as she had done years previously to secure what became the Lisbon Treaty. The problems facing the EU were enormous, help was not coming from the outside, and the Union itself was too weak to deal with them. Business and civil society groups, long present at the EU level, began to lobby for a great leap forward in European integration. It was redolent of the forces that built up in favour of the single market in the early 1980s, except this time leadership came from the European Council, not the Commission, and the range of interest groups involved included charities, local authorities and grassroots organisations.

In early 2019, President Merkel established a new Constitutional Convention on the basis of members nominated by each member state, which produced a text within eight weeks. Accepted by a majority of 75% in a referendum across the nearly 40 states of the EU, the Constitution came into force in 2021 – even the UK, smarting from the loss of East Anglia to the rising North Sea, had voted in favour. After a pan-European election, a new European Parliament (EP) was elected, and President Merkel became the leader of the first European government – a coalition between her own European People's Party, which had become devoted to sustainable development, following the lead of both Merkel herself and the UK's Conservatives, and the Greens. The European Federation had been born.

BOX 7.1: KEY LEARNING POINT – NEOFUNCTIONALISM

Neofunctionalism is the most well-known theory of European integration. It was established by scholars in the 1950s, who wanted to explain why and how the member states had agreed to reduce their independence and undertake what neofunctionalists understood to be a slow but sure path to a United States of Europe. Neofunctionalists thought that the process of European integration would be pushed forward by three main factors. First, the EU institutions themselves, which would have an interest in deepening integration in order to acquire more power. Second, interest groups and businesses, which would see benefits from taking part in a wider market and seek to shape the new system to suit themselves. Third, a process known as 'spillover', whereby integration in one area of policy leads to calls for integration in a linked area of policy, so that the maximum gains from integration in the first area could be had. For example, if the EU has powers in foreign policy it might be logical also to give it powers in defence policy, because otherwise the union would not be able to enforce its objectives.

There is some worth in the neofunctionalist model. The EU has clearly developed over time, and acquired further powers. However, neofunctionalists chose the wrong actors as the principal catalysts of integration. Although much evidence of influence by interest groups and the EU institutions can be found, and spillovers have at times occurred, the main powers in the EU have always been held by the member governments, which have resisted many attempts to deepen integration when it did not suit them. Nonetheless, in recent years, the deepening of the EU has made scholars re-examine neofunctionalism.

For key neofunctionalist work, see Ernst Haas (1964, 1968) and Leon Lindberg and Stuart Scheingold (1971). On its revival, see Rosamond (2000) and Wiener and Diez (2004).

The European Latticework

The ratification of the Lisbon Treaty proved to be a turning point in the European integration process. The only state to hold a referendum on the Treaty, Ireland, initially voted against the Treaty. After much soul-searching, the necessary changes were negotiated, giving Ireland a complete opt-out from the ESDP, and ensuring that the EU could only ever set tax rates for Ireland with the express permission of Irish citizens, to be obtained in a special referendum. In 2011, the Treaty was finally put on the statute book after a three-year ratification process.

Clearly, the EU could no longer easily agree on a way forward that would suit all its members equally. Successive Treaties since Maastricht had increased the range and number of opt-outs given to particular states, and even at the intergovernmental level it was proving almost impossible to generate a uniform view of the EU's big picture. An EU of 31 member states – Croatia having joined in 2010, followed by Bosnia, Macedonia and Serbia in 2011, as the EU looked for a 'good news story' about itself – simply could not deal with the questions of the Union's *finalité politique*, or ultimate end-point, as well as it could deal with the daily round of law-making. Even at that level, the increasing diversity of the Union in terms of its component states' political histories, cultures, policy preferences, and economic development levels, not to mention the often bitter relations between some of their politicians, made things increasingly difficult: the most well-recognised image of the EU ever was the capture by CNN of the moment when the irate Bosnian Foreign Minister, Dragana Vukovic, slapped her Serbian equivalent, Ratko Jankovic, in the middle of a press conference on Europe Day (May 9th), 2013. It became an instant YouTube classic.

The only way forward for the Union seemed to be based on promoting the idea of flexibility as the core principle of its constitutional settlement. Of course, both citizens and elites had long been concerned about subsidiarity, in other words about how much power should be transferred to the Union, and in which policy areas. However, beyond this general will to ensure something viable remained of national sovereignty, there was much less agreement; some member states, such as Belgium, remained keen for the EU to become a federation, but others, such as Greece and Serbia, were completely opposed to such a step-change. Even among the federalists, there were differences: Germany wanted a common European foreign policy, but also wanted to locate that clearly in an Atlantic alliance; France wanted such a common foreign policy, but also to use it as a means of greater independence from Washington.

Furthermore, the state systems of the EU remained very different; it was true that administratively, common cultures, processes and even values were being deepened across bureaucracies in the Union's states, but that did not amount to harmonisation of state structures or relationships between the centre and periphery in the member states. These relations continued to range from federalism in states such as Austria, to ongoing devolution (the UK, where Scotland had gained further powers in the dying days of the Labour government in 2010), to near-total monopoly of power by central governments (Luxembourg). This meant that EU policies had to be implemented differently according to national conditions and possibilities, and these differences grew with every enlargement of the Union.

Still more tellingly, a European political identity was still at best part-formed. The turnout for the EP elections of 2009 and 2014 continued to decline. There was no healing of the split in political values between those states broadly seeking to use the EU to promote social democracy – the Nordic bloc, France, in its strange neo-Gaullist variant, and Spain – and those seeking to use it to lock-in the free market system: the UK, Poland, Portugal, and the Baltic states. Germany played a frequent role as mediator between the two camps, aided by the President of the European Council, Angela Merkel, who had at last been able to take up her post in 2012 after the final ratification of Lisbon. This tended to be easier on less important matters than on issues of further Treaty change, or regarding major new policies such as how to deal with the increasing numbers of migrants from Africa, seeking to escape the desertification and increasing descent into violence of large parts of that continent.

However, it remained very difficult for the member states to accept the need for flexibility as a core principle of the EU, rather than as a handy solution to particular problems. For the federalists, it was seen as akin to the end of the dream, because a flexible Europe would be one in which some member states would always be less 'European' than others; for the more national sovereignty-conscious states, flexibility was an acceptance that the Union might develop in ways they did not want, and a dog-in-the-manger mindset prevented London and Warsaw extending the same courtesy to other member states that they had received themselves over the single currency (Poland had insisted on receiving the same treatment as Sweden regarding accession to the euro; Stockholm had no formal opt-out, but joining the euro was still so unpopular in Sweden that no government could enforce it and hope to survive).

Thus, by 2018 the Union was pretty much the same as it had been in 2008, with the exception of the institutional changes that had finally been implemented after 2011. The EAS was functioning smoothly, and so was the euro – which now included 23 states. There had even been agreement on climate change, but this resulted not so much from solidarity but from a wish to shape the global agenda; the Union's budget remained small, and there was little exchange of cash between richer and poorer member states to address the need to re-think the economy for a carbon-neutral world, but in a dizzying diplomatic coup the Union had espoused a global leadership role in this area of policy, in alliance with China, and this agreement held firm in the face of continued US ambivalence.

However, in 2019 a crucial event occurred, somewhat unexpectedly. The newly-elected EP, under the leadership of the Finnish MEP Tarja Stubb, demanded the right to elect the Commissioners, not simply share in their election. Member states were divided on this issue; it was a clear claim to deepen Euro-federalism, and while some could support this, others could not. A crisis erupted since the EP simply refused to participate in the appointment process of the new Commission, leaving a legal and political void which could not be filled. The ECJ confirmed in *Poland and Serbia versus European Parliament* (2020) that the member states had no choice; under the existing Treaties, they simply had to involve the EP in the process. This ruling split the European Council; and after a further year of negotiations brokered by acting Council President Willy Clijsters, a new Treaty was agreed in Ljubljana and put to an EU-wide referendum, as well as national ratification procedures, in 2021.

The FET, or Flexible Europe Treaty, received widespread support, and became law with ease. It made the EU more complex, but more legitimate, since there was much less need for states to adopt policies that they did not really want. The EU did not split into fragments either; all states wanted to participate in the single market, and with almost 30 states in the euro-zone, the currency remained stable. The Charter of Fundamental Rights provided a core baseline of common principles, and had been legally enforceable for over a decade. However, the Stability and Growth Pact was altered to allow greater public spending by euro-zone states, and as a result a dozen member states deepened their cooperation in social policy. While Britain led a group of member states seeking to privilege the Atlantic Alliance, France led a group which developed a European Defence Policy; force of necessity meant that other issues of foreign policy, under-pinned by the pre-existing agreement with China over climate change issues, were capable of joint approaches, particularly given the reinforcements made to the role of the EU High Representative under the Ljubljana Treaty. The EU's institutions made policy only for states which chose to accept Union competence in a given issue area, and although this did cause regular turf battles and disputes regarding the Union's legal competences, the new Court of Competences and Flexibility, established by the Ljubljana Treaty, was quickly able to establish its authority. The EU was even able to think creatively about extending its policies to non-member states, thereby reinforcing its most successful external policy of the previous century, enlargement. When Iceland and Norway joined the euro, but not the EU, in 2022, it seemed that the Union had finally found a way to act as the central point of a working pan-European governance system.

Residual Europe

By 2009, it became quite clear that the Lisbon Treaty was not going to be ratified. The Irish had voted against it in their referendum, and demanded the same treatment as that given to their French and Dutch counterparts in 2005; Ireland had approved the Nice Treaty on a second referendum, but public opinion was so clear that it would not do the same for Lisbon, with even many of those who had voted

BOX 7.2: KEY LEARNING POINT –
THE 'CONDOMINIO' AND MULTI-LEVEL
GOVERNANCE

The concept of the 'condominio' was put forward by Philippe Schmitter in the mid-1990s. Schmitter had been among the neofunctionalist group of scholars in the 1970s, but sought a new way to understand the European integration process because, although the EU had by the 1990s acquired many further powers, it had failed to become a new federal state, and the member states themselves retained power in many key areas of policy. Schmitter wanted to understand why the member states are occasionally happy to increase the EU's powers, and even occasionally make sacrifices of sovereignty that had seemed very unlikely, but do not make the final step towards creating a new Euro-federation. He also wanted to understand the broader context of European integration, in which the EU is just the biggest cog in a bigger continental governance machine. Schmitter developed four possible models for the EU's future development, in an attempt to understand how the Union's development could best be conceptualised. He argued that the EU is such a novel kind of polity that we need a new set of concepts to describe it. Among these is the 'condominio': a messy set of overlapping European structures and institutions, with diverse memberships and different functions, which he contrasted with the traditional approach of neofunctionalism – the creation of a new federal state. See Schmitter (1996) and also Zielonka (2006).

Several scholars have begun to explore how the EU may be developing a similar kind of internally varied system, with different policy areas working according to different rules, and where power is shared (or fought over) between the different tiers of government – local, regional, national and European. These scholars have put forward the notion of 'multi-level governance'. For the key original article, see Marks et al. (1996).

'yes' arguing that to hold a second referendum would be morally wrong, that Brian Cowen, the Irish Taoiseach, had no choice but to let the Treaty fall. The ensuing crisis in the EU was without precedent, even in the context of the post-Nice years. A Constitutional Treaty had been drafted, rejected by the member states, re-drafted, rejected by citizens, and ultimately replaced by an ostensibly different Treaty after years of soul-searching. This Treaty had itself now bitten the dust. What on Earth could the EU do?

The euro-zone just about held off market panic, thanks to a still-weak US dollar and China's unwillingness to use the yuan to crush it. The single market continued to function, as countless businesses had become inter-linked and mutually dependent in the prior two decades, but the EU institutions ceased to function effectively. EP elections were duly held in 2009, and a new Commission appointed in something of a haze; but they had no real authority, and in the European Council frantic diplomacy was ongoing. COREPER became the centre of EU activity, because it was there that member states could rely on seasoned diplomats, used to working with each other and in the EU system, to move at least some issues forward.

That worked as far as uncontroversial policies went. But on issues that were controversial in any of the member states, there was hardly ever progress, because no national government wanted to be seen to make sacrifices for an EU that was so clearly in trouble. There was no question of increasing the EU budget, and indeed after elections in the UK and Ireland produced new governments determined to slash their respective contributions, the budget was cut dramatically. The Commission closed all its departments except those on energy, the environment, the single market, and external trade as it no longer had the resources to do anything else. The EP used its rules of procedure to reduce its number of committees to the same issue areas, with an additional committee for petitions (which received roughly thirty such documents in 2009–2014) as a token gesture at maintaining ties with the citizen. The ECJ ceased to hear cases on anything but the most mundane of matters, under clear political instructions from the European Council that it would otherwise be abolished. There had been no enlargements since 2007.

Sensing opportunities, China and the USA worked together over the 2010–2016 period to ensure that the global trade negotiations under the auspices of the World Trade Organisation (WTO) were successful, and even reflected terms that a weakening EU could accept. Russia was bought off by the proposal to create a new diplomatic body for the WTO, its own Commission, which would set its agenda on the basis of proposals from the USA, Russia and China, with invitations to temporary membership of this body extended to India, Brazil, and, alternating for each other, France and Germany.

The Beijing–Washington axis, developed by a US in economic difficulty and thus more prepared to engage with international organisations, and a China wanting to cement its peaceful acquisition of superpower status, left Brussels in no position to shape the agenda. That said, existing WTO rules gave it an effective veto power, and in what would be its last act of global influence the EU agreed a trade regime which deepened world market integration in a way which left the single European market as an accepted regional face of the emerging global regime, to be represented by France and Germany. The UK, increasingly Eurosceptic, had unilaterally pulled out of the Union in 2013, remaining in the European Economic Area but devoting its foreign policy attentions to links with Washington, Beijing and New Delhi rather than Brussels, Berlin or even Moscow. Ironically, this reduced London's perceived value in Washington, but as part of the USA's negotiating strategies in the WTO, the UK was invited to join NAFTA and did so in 2015. Linked to London by its common travel area and dense economic ties, not to mention their shared interest in peace in Northern Ireland, the Irish Republic finally chose Boston over Berlin in the same year.

The really tough decisions came in early 2019. EP elections were due in summer of that year, but increasing numbers of member states could not see the point. Citizens in many member states could not have cared less about the EP if they had tried; and even the remaining federally-minded states – the original six members, plus Spain and Portugal – considered the expense wasteful in the circumstances. Hence, the European Council cancelled the elections by proclamation in March 2019. This was the clearest signal imaginable that the integration process risked lapsing into a terminal condition, and, concerned about the impact on their economic and political security, the eight members of the federalist group negotiated the grounds for secession.

This splitting up of the EU made tangible what everyone in Brussels had known for a while: beyond the single market, there was little that many member states really wanted from the EU, at least in the contexts of continued American provision of security, and a more measured use of energy supply as a foreign policy tool by Moscow. As the global trade regime deepened, most European states sought economic safety in that, and the single market was becoming indistinguishable from its global equivalent by 2021 as France and Germany were sidelined in the WTO Commission. The last residue of the European integration project was the federation declared by Benelux, Germany, France, Italy, Spain and Portugal in 2020. Taking the euro as a shared currency, but renaming it the florin, and establishing Esperanto as its official common second language, the Union of European States (UES) weathered initial difficulties in the currency exchanges thanks to its deeply integrated and initially protectionist single market, and, by 2025, it had emerged as a force to be reckoned with on the world stage thanks to a major economic recovery. France and Germany had of course pooled their voices in the new WTO Commission and by 2025 the UES had secured a permanent seat there as the price for its full inclusion in the global trade regime.

BOX 7.3: KEY LEARNING POINT – 'INTERGOVERNMENTALISM'

'Intergovernmentalism' is an approach to European integration which has long been seen as the rival and alternative to neofunctionalism. It is descended from Realist thinking in international relations theory, and essentially argues that the member states retain all meaningful power in the EU, and will never allow themselves to become part of a European federation. Instead, states co-operate in the EU because they think that such co-operation suits their own interests: they get more done by collaboration than they would on their own, and they have better opportunities for economic growth through participation in a single European market than they would by trying unilaterally to compete in the world economy.

Intergovernmentalism was largely unchallenged during the 1970s, when the European integration process seemed to be stalling. However, when the process gained momentum again, intergovernmentalist scholars had to re-evaluate their approach in order to explain why a major step forward such as the single market had taken them by surprise. Recent work in the intergovernmentalist camp has been of two kinds.

First, Moravcsik's theory of 'liberal intergovernmentalism', in which European integration is explained as a two-level process in which national governments are the key actors. They are central at national level, because they decide what is the 'national interest', and they are central at EU level, because it is they who have to make bargains with other governments in order for the EU to make decisions. National governments are unwilling to delegate too many powers to the EU, and this places a limit on what European integration can achieve.

Second, 'confederal consociationalism', which holds that the EU has become an interesting kind of polity in which the member states remain key and in control of their most important powers, but in which they are bound together by a raft of rules, practices and shared interests. It would be too costly – both economically and in terms of national interest – to break up this set of rules and practices. Thus, European integration is unlikely to unravel. However, by the same token it is also unlikely to make any further great leaps forward, because the member states consider that further deepening of the EU's powers would cause their own undermining in ways which are too fundamental to allow.

For the chief work in liberal intergovernmentalism, see Moravcsik (1999). For an intriguing work on confederal consociation, see Chryssochoou (1994).

WHAT MIGHT CHANGE? ISSUES OF LIKELY IMPORTANCE

There are many issues that are likely to shape the future development of the EU. It is impossible to predict with pin-point accuracy exactly how the Union will evolve; it is similarly difficult to predict every factor that will have a significant impact on its evolution. Surprises have a way of occurring... Consequently, in this part of the chapter I look at those factors which appear, at the time of writing, to be most likely to impact importantly on the development of the Union in the coming decade or so. I highlight four issues outside the EU policy process (climate change, transatlantic relations, relations with Russia and relations with emerging economic powers), before turning to the domestic politics of the member states and then to key structural and policy issues in the EU itself.

External issues

* *Climate Change.* Although this is by no means an issue for the EU alone, climate change is likely to drive the EU's agenda in the

coming years. Optimistic scenarios argue that the EU can play a lead role in combating global warming, and arguably the EU is already doing this in terms of brokering international agreements and developing innovative policy tools, such as the Emissions Trading Scheme. Pessimistic scenarios, however, point to runaway climate change with the capacity to cause massive environmental damage, and associated social and economic calamities. If these scenarios are right, then to the extent that the EU continues to exist, it will have to devote its efforts to solving these problems, or at least managing their consequences as effectively as possible.

- *Relations with the USA*. With the arrival of the euro and the expansion of the single market across the continent of Europe, the Union has become a particularly powerful economic player on the world stage. Although there is some evidence that the USA and EU can find common (self-promoting) cause when it comes to dealing with the third world – as demonstrated at the Cancún WTO negotiations of 2003 – it is also clear that trade disputes between the USA and EU on issues such as genetically modified foods have grown in importance in recent years. Such differences of opinion have, however, been dwarfed by major divisions over foreign policy issues, especially but by no means uniquely during the Presidency of George W. Bush. The extent of this division should not be exaggerated; there is no sense that the transatlantic relationship is irreparably damaged. Nonetheless, the relationship between the USA and the EU is a key factor to watch in the Union's evolution because it has a direct bearing on the Union's standing, and role, in global politics. It is also the key to the development of EU competence in foreign and defence policy: if the USA either insists on maintaining the role of NATO in European security, or alternatively chooses to abandon NATO, the Union's need and capacity to build its own defence competences are reduced (in the first case) or enhanced (in the second). Will the USA continue to be the senior partner in European security? Will policy differences between the EU and the USA grow to such an extent that the Union decides to elaborate its own foreign and defence policies regardless of USA preferences?

- *Relations with Russia* are a further key issue for the EU in terms of its immediate evolution. Many citizens of the 2004/7 entrants to the Union continue to be wary of Russia, and see both EU and

NATO membership as the key to their own national security. The 2004 and 2007 enlargements also gave the Union a much greater border with Russia, not to mention member states with significant Russian minorities. The Union's foreign policy centre of gravity has certainly shifted eastwards in recent years, e.g. its successful intervention in support of the 'Orange Revolution' in Ukraine; however, future enlargements of the Union to other countries of the ex-USSR may further blur the line for many Russians between Union accession by former satellite states and that by countries they consider to be historically part of Russia itself. Handling relations with Russia is thus likely to be a key challenge, particularly in a context where Russian internal governance is increasingly authoritarian and the respective roles of Russia, the Union and the USA in both European and international security after the Cold War are still forming. Issues of energy supply are also crucial here, since many EU states are heavily reliant upon gas and oil from Russia.

- *Relations with China and India* are of vital concern for the EU as the century develops. China is developing into an economic superpower, and is in that regard rather like the EU, but one based on a single, and still authoritarian, state. As China takes a bigger role in global affairs, gazes will be turned on Beijing to establish its priorities and capacities. Whether Sino-EU relations develop into rivalry or a form of partnership will be a key factor in determining the EU's global role, particularly in the context of China's potential to provide an alternative sponsor for developing countries – a role the EU often claims for itself – and to constitute a pole of economic, and even military, power that commands attention from other global players. At the time of writing, relations between the EU and India receive less attention than those with China, but the emergence of India as a global player will also have an impact on the EU's external policy options, providing both a further potential partner but also a potential rival. Should tensions between India and China become excessive, this will also shape the context in which the EU has to operate outside its borders.
- *Developments in the Balkans* will be of great import to the EU. At the time of writing, relations between the EU and Serbia are strained, over the question of independence for Kosovo. The EU's

ability to deal with these tensions will be a crucial test of its external policy capacities, whether Serbia and the remaining other states from the former Yugoslavia, as well as Albania, eventually accede to the Union or not.

National factors

- *Domestic politics in the member states* will continue to play a vital role in shaping the Union, because what member governments consider the 'national interest' is largely shaped by national-level problems, issues and constraints. On an issue-by-issue basis, this can mean that member states take apparently illogical stands based on their previous records, as national politics shifts. For example, a national demonstration by a key interest group, or the intervention in the debate of a more senior cabinet member, might change the position taken by a national minister on a particular directive. On a more general basis, important events such as economic slowdowns or general elections can change national positions very radically. Thus, previously blocked waterways can become navigable, as after the election of Donald Tusk, who dropped Polish claims to opt-outs from the Charter of Fundamental Rights, to the premiership of Poland in 2007. However, previously 'done deals' can be unravelled, as with the 2007 election to the French Presidency of Nicolas Sarkozy, who insisted on re-visiting the balance between competition and social policy capacities in the Lisbon Treaty.
- *Devolution and secession in the member states.* Although nothing can be taken as given, it has for many years been suggested that the EU might provide a safe arena for currently stateless nations to claim independence because it can both protect its members against some of the ravages of globalisation and provide some of the key aspects of influence that small states are otherwise unlikely to have. Certainly, European integration has been accompanied by devolution in many of the member states, and although this has not cut national governments out of the picture it has in some cases given wider influence to actors at regional levels. Furthermore, the existence and success of many small states such as Ireland, Malta and Slovenia in the EU has often been taken to indicate small states might be more viable than

previously considered likely – a claim made repeatedly by Scottish nationalists, for example. 2007 was marked by the long failure to agree a new government in Belgium; months passed before the Walloon and Flemish communities could agree a deal. If such an experience is repeated, Belgium may well break up. If developments in other member states, such as the UK, are suitable, currently stateless nations, e.g. Scotland, may claim independence – although this does not currently appear likely, and it must be a moot point whether new states such as an independent Wallonia would automatically inherit EU membership.

Internal EU Issues

- The first internal issue of great salience is a basic one: *will the Lisbon Treaty be ratified?* The procedure for this is considered to be less onerous than that applied to the Constitutional treaty, since only one member state (Ireland) is holding a referendum. However, it may not be safe to assume that all twenty-six of the other national parliaments will accept the new Treaty; at the time of writing, Hungary has done so, but twenty-five more states have yet to take the plunge. If the Treaty of Lisbon is ratified, the institutional changes it contains contained will slowly become embedded, and the Union's development will proceed – institutionally speaking – as intended. If not, then the Union will in all likelihood experience a major crisis. It could perhaps continue to operate under its existing rules for some time, and the Nice Treaty, which would constitute the apex of Treaty reform if Lisbon fails, has managed to work more effectively than often anticipated. That said, after the collapse of the Constitutional Treaty, failure to ratify Lisbon would almost certainly plunge the EU's credibility to an all-time low, causing a major growth opportunity for therapists in Brussels.

- The next key factor is the perennial problem of money. The *EU budget* is very small, and the member states have set a limit on their contributions to it (1.06% of GDP for the period 2007– 2013). Current policies on agriculture and regional development are simply impossible to continue under their current rules because they would bankrupt the Union – unless, of course, the richer member states agree to pay more into the EU coffers. Such member states are currently extremely reluctant to do this, and budget discussions over the next few years will be extremely interesting to observe on many counts. Will the new member states get equal treatment with pre-2004 members? Will the size of the budget be increased to pay for progress in areas such as foreign and defence policy, or could this come from an end to the British rebate and a 'repatriation' of farm subsidies? How will the budget be drawn – will there be a direct payment in the form of a tax from the citizen?

- The functioning of *the euro* is a further important factor. Heavily criticised in its first two years for being a 'weak' currency on the foreign exchange markets, how will the strengthening euro actually perform regarding the promotion of economic growth in the euro-zone? With the Stability and Growth Pact already undermined at the time of writing, since both France and Germany have cavalierly disregarded it in the face of domestic pressure, will the euro policy regime be reformed, and possibly even pool more sovereignty to maximise the external policy influence for the euro-zone states/the EU? Now with 15 members, will the euro-zone continue to work effectively? Will the member states that have currently opted out reverse their decisions?

- A further concern is the *'democratic deficit'*. Although there are many interpretations of this term, it essentially comprises two parts: an institutional aspect, and a political identity aspect. Will institutional reform succeed? If so, will it persuade EU citizens that the Union governs in a legitimate way? Will EU citizens develop a greater sense of belonging together with each other in the Union? Or will they continue to be rather detached from the Union, with a default position of either apathy or cynicism? Will the increased freedom of movement rights of recent years, and their more frequent invocation by citizens seeking holidays, second homes, permanent relocation, or jobs, make the nationals of each member state feel they have more, or less, in common with each other? And if so, how will this affect the capacity of EU elites to take radical action on EU reform if they so wish?

- A further issue is that of managing *the impact of the 2004 and 2007 enlargements*. The practical costs of Union governance have risen, as translation and interpretation requirements have grown rapidly. A more important issue thrown up by enlargement, however, is that of how the 2004 and 2007 entrants will envision the Union. Since 2004, it has become apparent that there is no monolithic 'Eastern bloc' in the EU, but at least one of the recent states – Poland – has enjoyed making itself quite as awkward as the UK, Greece, Sweden and France. Will the EU be able to repeat its past successful enlargements beyond 2007? If so, will this include accession by Turkey?

• A final issue to consider is that of *flexibility*. Will the member states continue to try to take action on a whole-EU basis? Or do the examples of monetary union and the Rapid Reaction Force indicate that the Union's way forward is to assemble coalitions of the willing? Certainly, as the number of member states rises, it becomes increasingly unlikely that all of them will want to participate in each key Union policy, especially as many of the areas in which the EU still has few powers are those, such as tax and defence, which lie at the heart of the member states' remaining sovereignty. Thus, the key question is whether member states will be happy to accept that progress made by some of them is better than no progress at all – and conversely, whether other member states will accept that their right to opt out is sufficient, or whether they need to use their veto to make sure there is no EU action in policy areas they would rather keep exclusively national.

CONCLUSIONS: TOWARDS A EUROPEAN LATTICEWORK?

The coming years seem likely to keep the EU on a similar trajectory to its current course, which is to say that it is likely to keep muddling through. There is no sign that member states want to be rid of the Union, or to return to the kind of continental politics which preceded the Second World War. Many of the member states are not eager to see the EU become a federation in its own right, but by the same token all of them consider it a useful device for solving policy problems. So, while a future such as *Residual Europe*, in which the Union collapses and is replaced by a mixture of deeper global regimes and a federation of a small number of its current states, cannot be ruled out, it does not appear to be what national elites really want.

Nor does it seem that a European Federation will spring into being in the short or medium term. Although there has clearly been huge deepening – and widening – of the Union since its inception, the member states have also proved entirely capable of resisting changes and developments to which they are fundamentally opposed. Even the Draft Constitutional Treaty that was rejected by member governments in 2003 did not propose the creation of a EU state with a single federal government. It is very unlikely that such an arrangement would occur in the short term through accumulated pressures from successful integration in key sectors, or because it could simply be a sensible next step in order to maximise the benefits that could be gained: for example, member states have been quite happy to have a European Central Bank, but have also been just as happy to keep control of fiscal and taxation policy as an essentially domestic matter.

So, while it must be possible that one day the EU will become a federation, if this happened soon it would really be against the run of play. Instead, the member states have been much happier to create particular policy regimes which might be described as federal, if by that we mean that national sovereignty has effectively been abandoned, in a narrow range of areas, and treat others as matters of entirely national preserve, while sharing sovereignty with the Union on a messy and changeable basis in other areas. Although all federations have a balance of powers between centre and periphery, and thus do not address all policy areas centrally, the diversity of the Union's institutional arrangements and decision rules, in addition to the member states' continued will to place limits on the transfer of sovereignty to Brussels, Luxembourg, Strasbourg and Frankfurt, indicates that without a major crisis which causes a fundamental review of member state viability, national capitals are not, for the most part, willing to subsume themselves in a new Euro-state.

Thus, the remaining scenario, the *European Latticework*, is the only one still standing. Although events are unlikely to turn out in exactly the way I have described above, this scenario remains the most likely for the Union, since it reflects the probable increased salience of difference between the preferences and agendas of the member states and the continuing resistance of many of them to great steps forward in the political integration process. It assumes that much of the present *acquis* is here to stay, and that there is not likely to be much 're-patriation' of competences that have been transferred to the EU. This reflects what happens in the real-world European integration process: there are interesting plans to make agricultural subsidies a national matter again as a means to help reduce the EU budget and reform the Common Agricultural Policy, but in general matters tend to stay Europeanised once that process has taken root.

However, this scenario also assumes that further deepening of the Union's powers is likely to be very difficult. Over the last few years, it has been demonstrated that reaching agreement about Treaty change is increasingly hard, for several reasons. First, the number of states involved now is much larger than in the past, and logically it must be easier to agree when there are only six perspectives on a new Treaty than when there are twenty-seven. Second, the issues involved are now often closer to the heart of national sovereignty than in the past. This holds true both symbolically, for example EU citizenship, or the euro, and practically: again, the euro is an example, but many others, such as the EAS, could be mentioned. Thus while it is not impossible to find an agreement between national elites, the chances are that for many of them it will be increasingly harder to support further transfer of sovereignty to the EU – hence the more frequent talk of 'red lines' and 'emergency brakes' that can be used to prevent a member state being corralled into Europeanising an aspect of policy it wants to keep outside the Union's bailiwick. In this regard, the recent emphasis on Europeanising energy policy is both significant and unusual, since it is potentially the first major area of policy to be transferred to the Union since Maastricht.

The third reason why deepening the Union is likely to be more problematic in future is the EU's legitimacy crisis. The time of the so-called 'permissive consensus', when the citizens of the Union's states were largely willing to let the process continue above their heads, has been swept away by the EU's deepening and increasing diversity. National referenda on treaty change since the Single European Act – that is, for over 20 years – have been very controversial, and have now not only delayed Treaty ratification considerably (the SEA, Maastricht, Nice), but even stopped it altogether (the Constitutional Treaty). Thus, to deepen the Union further, it will be necessary to get the support of its citizens, and in all probability that is much likelier in some countries (Belgium, Spain, Germany) than others (the UK, Poland).

So, the key to the EU's future seems to be how it will make good its slogan of unity in diversity, particularly regarding the use of flexibility or 'enhanced cooperation'. This approach, which allows policy to be made by what might be called coalitions of the willing, has the potential to allow the Union to function as a coordinating device for the governance and security of the whole continent, but it also presents a core challenge to both federalist and intergovernmentalist ideas about what the EU should be. It also, however, reflects the way in which the EU has really been working for many years, given that neither the euro nor the ESDP would have been possible had it been required that all member states should participate, and given that Romania and Bulgaria have effectively been second-tier members in many ways in the initial part of their membership, during which they are under continued surveillance by the Commission regarding their full transition to liberal democracy. EU history shows that the majority of member states, most of the time, prefer incremental change to radicalism. They prefer to use the EU only when they have to, and to limit its actions as far as possible. The result of such calculations changes over time, as both domestic and international pressures lead states to re-calibrate the balance between 'national' and 'European' competence in a given policy area. Nonetheless, most member states continue to want European integration on the cheap.

It is not likely at the moment that the Union will come out of the closet about this.

An overt, official and clear break with the traditional understanding of the in itself largely undeclared end-goal of European integration – namely that all member states must proceed together towards a federal future – will be unacceptable to the pro-deepening member states until they have become thoroughly frustrated with the ability of other member states to impede their plans. Instead, whatever use is made of flexibility will probably rely in the medium term on the multi-speed idea – the notion that all member states want to adopt the same legislation, but some of them may take longer than others either to see its benefits or to be technically ready to adopt it. This idea appears to be mistaken given the continuing diversity of member state preferences – but to judge from current evidence it will take quite some time for many of the member states and the EU institutions to accept this.

Thus, by 2025 we are likely to have moved further towards a 'European Latticework', where complexity is the price paid for innovation, but exactly how far we will have gone depends largely on two things. First, the extent to which pro-integration member states are ready to think overtly about revising the Monnet Method, and the extent to which other member states are prepared to let them. Second, the extent to which global events, as well as those inside the member states, do not conspire to throw the Union off this trajectory by producing a crisis big enough for a fundamental re-think.

The Basics about the European Union continue to be fascinating. As the Union develops, it challenges our understandings of what an international organisation can be and do, and is fundamentally changing what it means to be a nation state on the continent of Europe. The EU also has its own pathologies and problems, its own limits and shortcomings. Recent years have made the process of European unification increasingly controversial, and increasingly complex. If there is a third edition of this book, I very much doubt that at least *that* part of the Union's story will be much different.

THINK POINTS

- What are the attitudes of the various member states towards increasing the powers and roles of the EU?
- What are the benefits and disadvantages of a federal United States of Europe?
- What are the major factors which will shape how the EU develops in the next few years? Do you think external, or internal, factors will be most influential in shaping the EU's future? Why?
- Which future for the EU would you prefer, and why?

FURTHER READING

Rosamond, Ben (2000) *Theories of European Integration* (London: Macmillan).
  The best single-authored guide to European integration theory available.

Schmitter, Philippe C. (1996) 'Imagining the Future of the Euro-Polity with the Help of New Concepts', in Gary Marks, Fritz W. Scharpf, Philippe C. Schmitter and Wolfgang Streeck (eds) *Governance in the European Union* (London: Sage).

A commentary on integration theory and an imaginative approach to understanding the EU and its future.

Therborn, Göran (1997) 'Europe in the Twenty-first Century: The World's Scandinavia?', in Peter Gowan and Perry Anderson (eds) *The Question of Europe* (London: Verso).
A provocative piece which puts European integration in the context of globalisation, and asks whether Europe's future is market-based integration or social democracy.

Wiener, Antje and Diez, Thomas (eds) (2004) *European Integration Theory* (Oxford: Oxford University Press).
A stimulating range of essays on the main strands of integration theory.

Zielonka, Jan (2006): *Europe as Empire: The Nature of the Enlarged European Union* (Oxford: Oxford University Press).
An intriguing re-thinking of the EU as a powerful but diverse entity based on overlapping jurisdictions and flexibility.

APPENDIX 1
INTERNET SOURCES OF INFORMATION ON THE EUROPEAN UNION

(i)   For *primary sources,* and up-to-date announcements on the EU, use the Union's own website: www.europa.eu

(ii) For *regular news and commentary* on EU matters, try www. euractiv.com

(iii) For *think tanks,* try the following:
    (a)   From a generally pro-EU perspective:
        European Policy Centre: www.epc.eu
        The Centre: www.thecentre.eu
        Centre for European Reform: www.cer.org.uk
        Federal Trust: www.fedtrust.co.uk
        Centre for European Policy Studies: www.ceps.be
    (b)   From a Euro-sceptic or more Euro-cautious perspective:
        The Bruges Group: www.brugesgroup.com
        Open Europe: www.openeurope.org.uk

(iv) For *academic analysis* of the EU, the best site is that of the University Association for Contemporary European Studies, or *UACES*. The UACES webpage is www.uaces.org. The free UACES on-line directory of academic experts is at: www. ExpertonEurope.com

(v)   Good *on-line academic journals* devoted to EU issues are:
The *Journal of Contemporary European Research*: www.jcer.net
European Integration On-line Papers: www.eiop.or.at

Finally, a word of caution: remember to be at least as critical with
your use of websites as with your use of printed documents.

APPENDIX 2
MEMBER STATES OF THE EUROPEAN UNION, AS ON 1 JANUARY 2008

MEMBER STATE	DATE OF ACCESSION	IN EURO?	FULL MEMBER OF SCHENGEN?
Austria	1995	Yes	Yes
Belgium	1952	Yes	Yes
Bulgaria	2004	No	No
Cyprus	2004	Yes	No
Czech Republic	2004	No	Yes
Denmark	1973	No	No
Estonia	2004	No	Yes
Finland	1995	Yes	Yes
France	1952	Yes	Yes
Germany	1952	Yes	Yes
Greece	1980	Yes	Yes
Hungary	2004	No	Yes
Ireland, Republic of	1973	Yes	No
Italy	1952	Yes	Yes
Latvia	2004	No	Yes
Lithuania	2004	No	Yes
Luxembourg	1952	Yes	Yes
Malta	2004	Yes	Yes

MEMBER STATE	DATE OF ACCESSION	IN EURO?	FULL MEMBER OF SCHENGEN?
Netherlands	1952	Yes	Yes
Poland	2004	No	Yes
Portugal	1986	Yes	Yes
Romania	2007	No	No
Slovakia	2004	No	Yes
Slovenia	2004	Yes	Yes
Spain	1986	Yes	Yes
Sweden	1995	No	Yes
United Kingdom	1973	No	No

GLOSSARY

ACP – African, Caribbean and Pacific countries. A group of former colonies of the member states, which have been the recipients of much of the EU's development aid.

acquis communautaire (or simply *'acquis'*) – the totality of EC legislation at any given time.

Amsterdam Treaty – treaty agreed by the member states in 1997, which made some progress in dealing with the so-called 'leftovers' from the Maastricht Treaty (q.v.). Perhaps the most notable reform implemented in the Amsterdam Treaty was the increase in power and influence it gave to the European Parliament (q.v.).

ASEAN – the Association of South-East Asian Nations. A regional organisation in South-East Asia. It is not so developed as the EU in institutional terms, but it has a lasting place in the international politics of South-East Asia and East Asia more generally.

Atlanticism – the belief that one's ends are best served through a close partnership with, and even reliance upon, the United States of America.

Benelux – Belgium, the Netherlands and Luxembourg. These three neighbouring states agreed a customs union between themselves in 1944. Since then, they have often been grouped together as 'Benelux' by commentators for the sake of convenience.

CFSP – Common Foreign and Security Policy, a key aspiration of the EU that was enshrined as one of its objectives by the Maastricht Treaty (q.v.).

Cold War – term used to denote the rivalry between the two super-powers of world politics after the Second World War, namely the USA and the USSR (q.v.). The Cold War came to an end with the collapse of communism (q.v.) in Eastern Europe in 1989 and the dissolution of the USSR in 1991.

Commonwealth – set up in 1931, this is an association of autonomous states which were formerly part of the British Empire. In the context of this book, its relevance is that the Commonwealth has often been considered by many Britons as a more obvious arena for UK involvement with other countries than the EU.

Communism – the political theory which holds that fair and just government can only come from the abolition of class differences, and from state (rather than private) control of the economy. The key communist thinkers were Karl Marx and Friedrich Engels. Communism became the official ideology of many states in the early-mid twentieth century, including the USSR (q.v.), and its satellite states in Central and Eastern Europe. At the time of writing, communism remains the nominal ideology of China.

Conditionality – the idea that development aid money or other grants will be given to a recipient state only if that state agrees to certain conditions set by the aid-giver. This means that states giving aid can have a big impact on the states they give it to; it is a key principle of both EU development policy and the enlargement process.

Convention on the Future of Europe – a body set up at the Laeken Summit of 2001 with the duty to prepare the ground for a new EU Treaty. It produced the Draft EU Constitution of 2003.

convergence criteria – a set of conditions which have to be met in order to qualify for membership of the euro. Established in the Maastricht Treaty (q.v.), the convergence criteria essentially seek to ensure that a country seeking to adopt the euro has low inflation, low interest rates, manageable levels of public debt and the ability to maintain the fixed exchange rate for its currency against other currencies in the euro-zone.

cordon sanitaire – otherwise known as a 'buffer zone', this is the idea that a state can protect itself from its enemies by controlling the geographical area close to, but outside, its own borders. Many considered Eastern Europe to constitute such a buffer zone for the USSR (q.v.) after the Second World War.

Council of Europe – Strasbourg-based organisation set up in 1949 to defend and promote human rights, democracy, the rule of law and a common European identity. Its main focus now is to help former Communist countries in their transition to liberal democracy (q.v.). The Council of Europe is *not* an EU institution, but rather is part of the web of organisations which have an important role in the governing of the European continent.

Council of Ministers – formally known as the Council of the European Union, this is the EU body which represents the national governments of the member states. It is the most powerful of the EU institutions.

customs union – the process by which countries agree to abolish barriers to trade between them (such as import taxes), and also to establish a common tariff to be imposed by all states in the customs union on imports coming from elsewhere. A customs union is an important stage in economic integration.

de Gaulle, Charles – President of France between 1958 and 1969. De Gaulle was a key figure in European integration, because his insistence upon the preservation of national sovereignty (q.v.) in the 'empty chair crisis' of 1965 placed severe limits on the possible growth of the EU for many years.

Delors, Jacques – President of the European Commission (q.v.) 1985–1995. Delors played a key part in the establishment of the single European market (q.v.), and was the Commission's most successful President.

democratic deficit – the idea that the way the EU works is insufficiently democratic. There are essentially two parts of this criticism. First, the argument that the EU policy-making process is not sufficiently open, participatory or accountable. Second, the argument that people do not feel European – they have no sense of European, rather than national or local, identity.

ECHR – European Court of Human Rights. This body sits in Strasbourg, and functions under the auspices of the Council of Europe.

EFTA – European Free Trade Association. Originally set up as a rival to the EU which would focus entirely on a limited form of economic integration, EFTA has in fact become an increasing irrelevance. Over time, most of its member states have abandoned it in favour of the EU.

Elysée Palace – official residence of the French President.

EMU – Economic and Monetary Union. The process by which the EU has established and adopted its own currency, the euro.

enlargement (or 'widening', or 'accession') – the process by which the EU takes in more member states. In terms of semantics, 'enlargement' tends to be used by people in existing member states, whereas 'accession' tends to be used by people in countries in the process of joining the EU. The EU has enlarged six times in its history (1973, 1980, 1986, 1995, 2004, 2007).

European Commission – the institution of the EU which causes the greatest controversy, the Commission is both the EU's civil service and, in theory, its political heart. The Commission is headed by a 'College' of Commissioners, who are political figures with particular policy responsibilities. The great majority of Commission staff, however, are civil servants.

European Court of Justice (ECJ) – highest court of the European Union, with its seat in Luxembourg.

European Parliament (EP) – the only directly-elected institution of the EU, the Parliament brings together deputies from each member state. The Parliament is increasingly powerful as a legislator, and now shares power with the Council of Ministers (q.v.) in most policy areas.

Europeanisation – the process by which member states of the EU retain much of their independence but nonetheless evolve from their various different starting points towards more uniform policies and structures, using the EU as a tool to help this process gather speed.

Federation – a political structure in which previously independent states become legally subservient to a new centre, or in which the centre grants powers to the periphery, based on a formal constitutional agreement which clearly separates and limits the powers of both the centre and the periphery, and which can be changed only by their mutual agreement. Many countries have federal systems, including certain member states of the EU itself (e.g. Germany, Austria and Belgium). In the EU context, this idea has been extremely controversial, because pro-integrationists have often seen federation as the logical outcome of the integration process, but defenders of national sovereignty (q.v.) have seen federation as the end of national independence.

Flexibility – the idea that European integration might not produce an outcome that is the same for every member state, and that not every member state of the Union need take part in each EU policy. Simply put, the advantage of flexibility is that those member states which choose to take integration further than others can be free to do so. The disadvantage is that the EU might thereby become more complex and uneven. A good example of flexibility is the single currency, in which only 15 member states take part at the time of writing.

Fusion – a similar concept to Europeanisation, developed by Wolfgang Wessels. The 'fusion' concept holds that the member states have become structurally interwoven with each other, and with the EU institutions, as a strategy for self-preservation. By doing this, the member states have transformed themselves and sacrificed a degree of independence, but the result has been their continued ability to exist.

GDP – gross domestic product, i.e. the total financial value of the goods and services produced by a state in a given period.

Global reserve currency – the currency that is bought by states across the globe as a means of protecting their economies. Reserve currencies are bought by states as part of their exchange reserves, and also serve as a benchmark for pricing commodities, so that there is a standard means of tracking developments in a commodity's price.

Globalisation – the process by which the world has become far more inter-linked and interdependent, particularly in terms of economics and politics. Through globalisation, individual states are becoming less important, and arguably less powerful, whereas international businesses and companies are becoming more so. Globalisation is, as a consequence, very controversial. Its relevance here is that European integration can be seen as either part and parcel of the globalisation process or as a means to resist it.

IGC – intergovernmental conference. A summit meeting of heads of state or government, at which major decisions about the future direction of the EU are made. All EU Treaties must currently result from an IGC.

Intergovernmental – literally, between governments; used in EU studies as a term to denote the preponderance of national governments, as opposed to the influence of the EU's own institutions. For example, the CFSP (q.v.) is accurately described as an 'intergovernmental' policy, because it is the member states rather than the Commission, Court or Parliament of the Union which hold power in the area.

Intergovernmentalism – neofunctionalism (q.v.)'s rival theory of integration. Intergovernmentalists hold that the EU is essentially controlled by the member governments, and will never evolve beyond being a tool for states to use for their own ends. For intergovernmentalists, member states have all meaningful power in the EU, and will never allow the Union to become a federation.

juste retour – literally, 'fair return'– the idea that member states should get back from EU membership a financial gain which is at least equal to their respective contributions to the EU budget. In the past, the UK was the main source of claims for a 'juste retour'; in recent years, several states have made similar arguments, implying that it may be very difficult to increase the size of the EU budget.

Keynesianism – the notion that governments should intervene in the economy if necessary to stimulate growth.

Kyoto Protocol – an agreement made at the United Nations aimed at combating climate change, notorious as a result of the USA's failure to ratify it.

laissez-faire – literally, 'allow to do'. This is the notion that governments must not intervene in the economy, but must instead let the market police itself, if economic growth is to occur.

liberal democracy – the orthodox form of governance in the Western world. Liberal democracy requires limited government (i.e. legal limits to the powers of the state), representation (the ability of citizens to elect representatives who make policy choices on their behalf), legitimate opposition (the idea that it is entirely lawful to oppose those in power and argue for their replacement), a market economy (i.e. an economic system which the state does not control), and a free press (i.e. the right of the media to be critical of those in power without being punished for it). Much of the argument that the EU has a democratic deficit (q.v.) is based on the Union's lack of fit with aspects of liberal democracy.

Maastricht Treaty (Treaty on European Union) – treaty signed by the member states in 1990 in the eponymous Dutch town, and ratified in 1992. The Maastricht Treaty represents what is so far the biggest single step forward in European integration. It included, among other notable achievements, a timetable for the adoption of the single currency, the commitment that the EU should work towards a common foreign and security policy, and the new status of EU citizenship.

Macroeconomics – 'big picture' economics, involving action on important issues at the general (or system) level, and the general performance of the economic system as a whole. It is usually contrasted with 'microeconomics', which deals with individual goods or resources.

Marshall Plan – a package of aid named after US Secretary of State George Marshall, granted to European countries by the USA after the Second World War. The USSR (q.v.) prevented countries in its sphere of influence from accepting this aid, and thus all recipients were in Western Europe. 'Marshall Aid' helped re-establish the economies and state structures of Western Europe, and was given on the condition that recipient states had to co-operate with each other in order to spend it. As a result, the Marshall Plan was a key early stage in European integration.

Member state – a country which has officially joined the EU.

Monnet, Jean – perhaps the key figure in ensuring the European integration process took place, Monnet worked behind the scenes in the late 1940s and early 1950s to foster a Franco-German alliance in support of integration. Working with the French government minister Robert Schuman and German Chancellor Konrad Adenauer, Monnet fostered the development of the European Coal and Steel Community (ECSC), the first stage in the development of what is now the EU. He was the first President of the High Authority of the ECSC–the forerunner of the European Commission (q.v.).

Multilateral – literally, many-sided. The term is used to describe institutions or negotiations between several states and other parties.

NAFTA – North American Free Trade Area: an agreement dating from 1992, by which the USA, Canada and Mexico agreed to abolish barriers to trade between themselves. Generally seen as a response to the economic challenge posed to the USA by the Single European Market (q.v.), NAFTA demonstrated that as European integration deepens it may spark similar plans for regional integration in other parts of the globe.

NATO – North Atlantic Treaty Organisation: set up in 1949, the original purpose of NATO was to link the countries of Western Europe and Turkey with Canada and the USA in matters of defence. NATO's original purpose was to defend Western Europe during the Cold War (q.v.). However, with the collapse of communism, NATO's role has come into question–particularly as a result of the EU's own increasing, if still limited, role in defence matters, and with the accession to NATO of many Central and Eastern European countries.

Neofunctionalism – an important theory of European integration, which argues that the process works on the basis of incremental progress, cultivated by the EU's institutions and those groups in society which see benefit in the integration process. In neofunctionalism, integration in one policy sector will lead to integration in another, rather like a line of dominoes which can all be knocked down by setting the first domino in motion. Neofunctionalism was criticised in the 1970s and early 1980s, because integration did not seem to be making progress and the member states appeared to be both willing and able to resist it. However, since the Single European Act (q.v.), neofunctionalism has been somewhat re-instated, albeit in revised form.

Neo-Gaullism – politics and policies which are similar to those espoused by Charles de Gaulle (q.v.), the former rightwing President of France who advocated an intergovernmental form of European integration which would nonetheless allow its member states to act independently of the USA in terms of foreign policy.

Neoliberalism – the economic theory which holds that the state should have little or no role in the economy, that inflation must be kept low, and that the market should be allowed a virtually free reign. Like globalisation (q.v.), neoliberalism is controversial in European integration because it has both helped take the process further along and made it focus on economic rather than social integration.

Nice Treaty – Treaty agreed in 2000, which made very little progress in the process of EU reform, but which did manage to include an agreement about how many votes each member state (q.v.) should have in the Council of Ministers (q.v.), and how many members of the European Parliament (q.v.) should be allowed for each member state, after the enlargement (q.v.) of 2004.

OECD – Organisation for Economic Co-operation and Development. Originally set up as a means for the allocation of Marshall Plan (q.v.) money, it metamorphosed into a body concerned with issues of economic development across Europe and beyond. OECD members have included non-European states such as the USA, Canada and Japan for several decades. The OECD is *not* an EU institution, but rather is part of the web of organisations which have an important role in the governing of the European continent.

OSCE – Organisation for Security and Co-operation in Europe. This body was set up in 1973, and has its main seat in Vienna. Its role is to help prevent international conflicts, manage international crises, and help rehabilitate states once they have emerged from conflict. It has 55 member countries, drawn from Europe, Central Asia and North America. The OSCE is *not* an EU institution, but rather is part of the web of organisations which have an important role in the governing of the European continent.

Ostpolitik – literally, 'Eastern policy'. The term was coined to describe West German attempts to relieve the tensions between itself and East Germany during the Cold War in the years following 1969. It was originally associated with former German Chancellor Willy Brandt.

Petersberg Tasks – the tasks for which the EU may use military forces. They focus on humanitarian activities, peace-keeping and peace-making.

Protectionism – the idea that a state's economic interests are best served by the prevention of free trade, or at least by the granting of significant advantages to domestic companies and firms.

public goods – those goods and services to which every member of a particular group (or even of a nation, or the human race) are entitled, whether he/she has contributed to their production or not. Public goods can be seen positively, as instances of the general interest, e.g. clean air. However, public goods can also be seen negatively, i.e. as goods which permit 'free-riding'–piggy-backing on the work of others.

qualified majority voting (QMV) – the procedure whereby member states vote in the Council of Ministers (q.v.). Qualified majority voting rules currently require that a legislative proposal be supported by member states which between them possess roughly 70% of the votes. Basically, QMV is a compromise between unanimity (where every member state must agree), and a 'simple majority' (in which anything over 50% of the vote is required). If the Lisbon Treaty is ratified, the rules for QMV will change in 2014, to require 55% of the member states (on a one state, one vote) basis, provided that these states also represent 65% of the EU population.

Rapid Reaction Force – the first security force of the EU, agreed in November 2000. It is not a standing army, but rather a commitment by the member states to provide up to 60,000 troops for an EU force which would undertake humanitarian, peace-keeping and crisis-management tasks when NATO (q.v.) has declared its unwillingness to be involved. Essentially, the RRF is a device whereby the member states (and their soldiers) can work together as Europeans, rather than as members of a broader international force. However, the RRF is, for the moment at least, clearly subordinate to NATO.

Second World War – massive military conflict between 1939 and 1945, which pitted Nazi Germany, Japan and, until the dying months of the conflict, Italy against a grand alliance of the USA, the Soviet Union (q.v.), and the UK. The destruction caused by this war was horrendous and helped create the drive towards European integration, as both a means to ensure peace and a means to re-create European economies.

sectoral co-operation – collaboration by the member states in specific areas (or 'sectors') of policy, often in the hope that co-operation in one policy area would lead to co-operation in related policy areas. This was the idea of Jean Monnet (q.v.), and has close links with neofunctionalism (q.v.).

Single European Act (SEA) – an agreement by the member states (q.v.) to increase their economic integration and create a single market for goods, services, capital and labour. The SEA was agreed in 1986, and included certain key institutional reforms such as qualified majority voting (q.v.) as the price to pay for the creation of the single market.

Single European Market (SEM) – the 'internal market' of the EU represents a deepening of economic integration beyond the customs union (q.v.). In the SEM, barriers to trade, and freedom of movement between EU states, are abolished in the attempt to foster economic growth.

social democracy, socialism – the belief that the market economy must be complemented (but not entirely replaced) by government action to ensure that the gaps between rich and poor do not become too wide.

sovereignty/national sovereignty – the ability of a state to determine and pursue its own course of action, with no other state or force being able to impose limits or constraints upon that action.

Soviet Union/USSR – the multi-national state, nominally a federation, set up by the Communist Party after the Russian Revolution of 1917. The Soviet Union collapsed in 1991 along with communist rule. The acronym USSR means Union of Soviet Socialist Republics. The main successor state of the USSR is Russia.

Subsidiarity – the principle that political decisions should be taken at the lowest possible level for efficiency. Subsidiarity has been extremely controversial in EU politics because for some proponents the 'lowest possible level' is the member state, whereas for others the lowest possible level might in some circumstances be the EU itself – or even local and regional governments.

Supranational – literally, above the national. In EU studies, the term refers to the EU level, and can imply that the EU level is more powerful than the national level.

Technical transfer – help given by one state (or actor) to another which involves helping the recipient develop new or more effective skills and technologies. This is a feature of development policy, and is increasingly central to the debate on climate change.

Third countries – countries which are not members of a particular organisation or not involved in a particular relationship. Thus, EU relations with 'third countries' would include those it has with South Africa or Israel, to give just two examples.

transnational polity – a political system which is composed of and modifies, but does not eradicate, individual member states. See also Europeanisation, fusion.

welfare state – the idea that a government should provide certain services to its citizens in order to ensure their basic welfare needs are met. These services would typically include education, health and social security.

WTO – World Trade Organisation, set up in 1995 and based in Geneva. A global body to facilitate free trade, it also has a dispute settlement mechanism which has seen the EU and USA clash on many trade issues.

Yalta – port on the Black Sea, now in Ukraine, where in 1945 Europe was divided into two spheres of influence by the USA and the USSR (q.v.).

NOTES

1 INTRODUCTION

1 An exception is the area of monetary policy, where the European Central Bank plays a highly important role. Decisions of the European Court of Justice are often also important in determining the boundaries of EU competence.

2 Since the Maastricht Treaty of 1992, all nationals of the EU's member states have been citizens of the EU as well as their state of origin. So, one is both Finnish and 'European', Bulgarian and 'European' and so on.

2 THE EVOLUTION OF EUROPEAN INTEGRATION

1 The following paragraphs draw heavily on Warleigh 2003, Chapter 2.

2 Exceptions were Yugoslavia and Albania (Davies 1997: 1100–04).

3 This claim persisted despite both the often severe tensions between China and the USSR, which led certain communist states to consider China rather than the Soviet Union as the head of the communist bloc.

4 For excellent guides to the UK's difficult relationship with the EU, see George (1994) and Young (1998).

5 This may not sound very impressive. However, as Burns (2002) shows, the cooperation procedure marked the beginnings of the European Parliament's path to real legislative power, and was thus a crucial first step.

3   INSTITUTIONS AND DECISION-MAKING IN THE EUROPEAN UNION

1   This section addresses the roles and functions of the EU institutions as they stand prior to the ratification of the Treaty of Lisbon, since at the time of writing such ratification cannot be taken for granted. The principal changes that would be introduced by the Treaty if it is successfully ratified are discussed in Chapter 6.

2   Another body, the European Council, has more power in terms of setting the EU's overall agenda. This body is composed of the heads of government of each member state. It meets only a few times a year, but it is this body which produces the EU Treaties. The European Council has also been used increasingly to resolve particularly difficult problems that the EU Council has been unable to address successfully.

3   Since the Maastricht Treaty, member states have been able to send politicians from regional rather than national governments to represent them in Council. However, in such cases it should be noted that regional ministers must represent the national government rather than their own region, or even the regional tier of government in their home state.

4   The EP shares the power to nominate the Commission President with the Council, and the power to appoint the College of the Commission with both the Council and the Commission President. It appoints the Ombudsman on its own.

4   KEY POLICIES OF THE EUROPEAN UNION

1   The phenomenon of flexible integration has much to recommend it as a way out of this trap (Warleigh 2002). However, as yet the rules for flexibility, or 'enhanced cooperation', make it difficult to operate, and rule out its use as a means of adding to EU competence in day-to-day legislation.

2   Regulation implies rule-setting, rather than the creation of new common policy as such. See the work of Giandomenico Majone (1996).

3   Nor do I present what follows as a definitive categorisation of the EU's responsibilities. Some observers, for example, would see freedom of movement as a key EU policy in its own right; I have treated it instead as a key component of both the Single Market programme and social policy.

6   CONTROVERSIES IN TODAY'S EUROPEAN UNION

1   See Chapter 4, Section III.

2   This is another reason why in recent years the EU has developed as a regulator, and as a maker of soft policy, rather than as a producer of detailed and binding legislation. Regulation and soft policy not only preserve national sovereignty rather more clearly than other forms of legislation; they also come cheaper.

3   For an initial attempt to do this, see the Commission's important but ultimately myopic White Paper on European Governance (2001).
4   For example, the new rules on QMV would not fully apply until 2014; similarly, the number of Commissioners will not be reduced until that date.

7   WHERE NOW FOR THE EUROPEAN UNION?

1   This judgement created the doctrine of 'direct effect', which means that member state nationals can use the rights they have under EC law to which the principle applies directly in national courts. Unlike traditional international law, there is no need for the member state to pass enacting legislation; the fact of the right's existence in EC law is enough. This 'direct effect' doctrine is a key part of the innovative character of EC law.

REFERENCES

Alter, K. and Meunier-Aitsahalia, S. (1994) 'Judicial Politics in the European Community: European Integration and the Pathbreaking Cassis-de-Dijon Decision' (*Comparative Political Studies* 26:4, 535–61).

Avery, G. *et al.* (2007) *The People's Project? The New EU Treaty and the Prospects for Future Integration* (Brussels: European Policy Centre, available at: www.epc.eu, accessed 8/1/08).

Bache, I. (1998) *The Politics of European Union Regional Policy: Multi-level Governance or Flexible Gate-keeping?* (Sheffield: Sheffield Academic Press).

Bache, I. and Flinders, M. (eds) (2004) *Multi-Level Governance* (Oxford: Oxford University Press).

Baldwin, M., Peterson, J. and Stokes, B. (2003) 'Trade and Economic Relations', in J. Peterson and M. Pollack (eds) *Europe, America, Bush: Transatlantic Relations in the Twenty-first Century* (London: Routledge).

Balme, R. and Woll, C. (2005) 'France: Between Integration and National Sovereignty', in S. Bulmer and C. Lequesne (eds) *The Member States of the European Union* (Oxford: Oxford University Press).

Barnes, I. and Barnes, P. (1999) *Environmental Policy in the European Union* (Cheltenham: Edward Elgar).

Bellamy, R. and Warleigh, A. (1998) 'From an Ethics of Integration to an Ethics of Participation: Citizenship and the Future of the European Union' (*Millennium* 27:3, 447–70).

Börzel, T. (2002) 'Pace-setting, Foot-dragging and Fence-sitting: Member State Responses to Europeanization' (*Journal of Common Market Studies* 40:2, 193–214).

Bretherton, C. and Vogler, J. (2006) *The European Union as a Global Actor* (2nd edn) (London: Routledge).

Bulmer, S. (1996) The European Council and the Council of the European Union: Gatekeepers of a European Federal Order?' (*Publius: The Journal of Federalism* 26:4, 17–42).

Burns, C. (2002) 'The European Parliament', in A. Warleigh (ed.) *Understanding European Union Institutions* (London: Routledge).

Calleo, D. (2001) *Rethinking Europe's Future* (Princeton, NJ: Princeton University Press).

Carlsnaes, W. (2007) 'European Foreign Policy', in K.E. Jørgensen, M. Pollack and B. Rosamond (eds) *Handbook of European Union Politics* (London: Sage).

Chryssochoou, D. (1994) 'Democracy and Symbiosis in the European Union: Towards a Confederal Consoiciation?' (*West European Politics* 17:4, 1–14).

Church, C. and Phinnemore, D. (2002) *The Penguin Guide to the European Treaties: From Rome to Maastricht, Amsterdam, Nice and Beyond* (London: Penguin).

Cini, M. (2002) 'The European Commission', in A. Warleigh (ed.) *Understanding European Union Institutions* (London: Routledge).

Cini, M. (2006) *European Union Politics* (2nd edn) (Oxford: Oxford University Press).

Cram, L. (1997) *Policy-making in the European Union – Conceptual Lenses and the Integration Process* (London: Routledge).

Damro, C. and Luaces Mendéz, P. (2003) 'Emissions Trading at Kyoto: From EU Resistance to Union Innovation' (*Environmental Politics* 12:2, 71–94).

Davies, N. (1997) *Europe: A History* (London: Pimlico).

Dawisha, K. (1990) *Eastern Europe, Gorbachev and Reform* (2nd edn) (Cambridge: Cambridge University Press).

De Rynck, S. and McAleavey, P. (2001) 'The Cohesion Deficit in Structural Fund Policy' (*Journal of European Public Policy* 5:4, 615–31).

Delanty, G. and Rumford, C. (2005) *Rethinking Europe: Social Theory and the Implications of Europeanization* (London: Routledge).

Devuyst, Y. (1998) 'Treaty Reform in the European Union: The Amsterdam Process' (*Journal of European Public Policy* 8:4, 541–57).

Dinan, D. (1999) *Ever Closer Union: An Introduction to European Integration* (2nd edn) (Basingstoke: Macmillan).

Dinan, D. (2004) *Europe Recast: A History of European Union* (Basingstoke: Palgrave).

Dover, R. (2006) 'The EU's Foreign, Security and Defence Policies', in M. Cini (ed.) *European Union Politics* (2nd edn) (Oxford: Oxford University Press).

Dyson, K. (2008) 'Fifty Years of Economic and Monetary Union: A Hard and Thorny Journey', in D. Phinnemore and A. Warleigh-Lack (eds) *Reflections on European Integration* (Basingstoke: Palgrave).

Elgström, O. (2007) 'The European Union as a Leader in International Mulitlateral Negotiations: A Problematic Aspiration?' (*International Relations* 21:4, 445–58).

Europolitics (2007) *Treaty of Lisbon: Here is What Changes* (Brussels: Europolitics, available at: www.europolitics.info, accessed 8/1/08).

Forsyth, M. (1981) *Unions of States: The Theory and Practice of Confederation* (Leicester: Leicester University Press).

George, S. (1994) *An Awkward Partner: Britain in the European Community* (2nd edn) (Oxford: Oxford University Press).

George, S. (1996) *Politics and Policy in the European Union* (3rd edn) (Oxford: Oxford University Press).

Grabbe, H. (2006) *The EU's Transformative Power: Europeanization through Conditionality in Central and Eastern Europe* (Basingstoke: Palgrave).

Haas, E.B. (1964) *Beyond the Nation State: Functionalism and International Organization* (Stanford, CA: Stanford University Press).

Haas, E.B. (1968) *The Uniting of Europe: Political, Social and Economic Forces 1950–1957* (2nd edn) (Stanford, CA: Stanford University Press).

Hall, P. and Taylor, R. (1996) 'Political Science and the Three New Institutionalisms' (*Political Studies* 45, 936–57).

Hill, C. (1995) 'The Capability–Expectations Gap, or Conceptualising Europe's International Role', in S. Bulmer and A. Scott (eds) *Economic and Political Integration in Europe* (Oxford: Blackwell).

Hill, C. and Smith, M. (2005a) 'Acting for Europe: Reassessing the European Union's Place in International Relations', in C. Hill and M. Smith (eds) *International Relations and the European Union* (Oxford: Oxford University Press).

Hill, C. and Smith, M. (2005b) 'International Relations and the European Union: Themes and Issues', in C. Hill and M. Smith (eds) *International Relations and the European Union* (Oxford: Oxford University Press).

Hix, S. (2005) *The Political System of the European Union* (2nd edn) (Basingstoke: Palgrave).

Hobsbawm, E. (1994) *Age of Extremes: The Short Twentieth Century* (London: Abacus).

Hooghe, L. and Marks, G. (2001) *Multi-level Governance and European Integration* (Boulder, CO: Rowman and Littlefield).

Howarth, D. (2002) 'The European Central Bank', in A. Warleigh (ed.) *Understanding European Union Institutions* (London: Routledge).

Hudson, J. and Lowe, S. (2004) *Understanding the Policy Process: Analysing Welfare Policy and Practice* (Bristol: The Policy Press).

Hunt, J. (2002) 'The European Court of Justice and the Court of First Instance', in A. Warleigh (ed.) *Understanding European Union Institutions* (London: Routledge).

Jordan, A. and Schout, A. (2006) *The Coordination of the European Union: Exploring the Capacities of Networked Governance* (Oxford: Oxford University Press).

Kagan, R. (2004) *Paradise and Power: America and Europe in the New World Order* (London: Atlantic Books).

Kaiser, W. and Starie, P. (eds) (2005) *Transnational European Union: Towards a Common Political Space* (London: Routledge).

Keating, M. and Hooghe, L. (2001) 'By-passing the Nation State? Regions and the EU Policy Process', in J. Richardson (ed.) *European Union Power and Policy-making* (London: Routledge).

Leibfried, S. and Pierson, P. (2000) 'Social Policy', in H. Wallace and W. Wallace (eds) *Policy-making in the European Union* (4th edn) (Oxford: Oxford University Press).

Leonard, M. (2005) *Why Europe will Run the Twenty-first Century* (London: Fourth Estate).

Lindberg, L. and Scheingold, S. (eds) (1971) *Regional Integration: Theory and Research* (Cambridge, MA: Harvard University Press).

Lintner, V. (2001) 'European Monetary Union: Developments, Implications and Prospects', in J. Richardson (ed) *European Union Power and Policy-making* (London: Routledge).

Lord, C. and Harris, E. (2006) *Democracy in the New Europe* (Basingstoke: Palgrave).

Lundestad, G. (1986) 'Empire by Invitation? The United States and Western Europe, 1945–1952' (*Journal of Peace Research* 23:3, 263–77).

Magnette, P. (2005) *What is the European Union? Nature and Prospects* (Basingstoke: Palgrave).

Majone, G. (1996) *Regulating Europe* (London: Routledge).

Manners, I. (2002) 'Normative Power Europe: A Contradiction in Terms?' (*Journal of Common Market Studies* 40:2, 234–58).

Marin, A. (1997) 'EC Environment Policy', in S. Stavridis, E. Mossialos, R. Morgan and H. Machin (eds) *New Challenges to the European Union: Policies and Policy-making* (Aldershot: Dartmouth).

Marks, G., Hooghe, L. and Blank, K. (1996) 'European Integration from the 1980s: State-centric vs. Multi-level Governance' (*Journal of Common Market Studies* 34:3, 341–78).

Meunier, S. and Nicolaïdis, K. (2006) 'The European Union as a Conflicted Trade Power' (*Journal of European Public Policy* 13:6, 906–25).

Milward, A. (1992) *The European Rescue of the Nation State* (London: Routledge).

Moravcsik, A. (1991) 'Negotiating the Single European Act: National Interests and Conventional Statecraft in the European Community' (*International Organization* 45:1, 19–56).

Moravscik, A. (1999) *The Choice for Europe: Social Purpose and State Power from Messina to Maastricht* (London: UCL Press).

Morgenthau, H. (1948) *Politics among Nations: The Struggle for Power and Peace* (New York: McGraw-Hill).

Neunreither, K. (2000) 'The European Union in Nice: A Minimalist Response to a Historic Challenge' (*Government and Opposition* 36:2, 184–208).

Nuttall, S. (1992) *European Political Cooperation* (Oxford: Oxford University Press).

Olsen, J. P. (2002) 'The Many Faces of Europeanization' (*Journal of Common Market Studies* 40:5, 921–52).

Open Europe (2007) *A Guide to the Constitutional Treaty* (London: Open Europe, available at www.openeurope.org.uk, accessed 8/1/08).

Peterson, J. (1994) 'Subsidiarity: A Definition to Suit any Vision?' (*Parliamentary Affairs* 47:1, 116–32).

Phinnemore, D. and Warleigh-Lack, A. (eds) (2008) *Reflections on European Integration* (Basingstoke: Palgrave).

Piening, C. (1997) *Global Europe: The EU in World Affairs* (Boulder, CO: Lynne Rienner).

Pinder, J. (2003) 'Editorial: Really Citizens?' (*Federal Trust EU Constitution Project Newsletter* 1:4, 1–3).

Pollack, M. (1995) 'Regional Actors in an Intergovernmental Play: The Making and Implementation of EC Structural Policy', in C. Rhodes and S. Mazey (eds) *The State of the European Union, Vol. 3* (Boulder, CO: Lynne Rienner).

Pond, E. (2004) *Friendly Fire: The Near-death of the Transatlantic Alliance* (Washington, DC: Brookings Institution Press/EUSA).

Pryce, R. (1994) 'The Maastricht Treaty and the New Europe', in A. Duff, J. Pinder and R. Pryce (eds) *Maastricht and Beyond: Building the European Union* (London: Routledge).

Radaelli, C. (2006) 'Europeanization: Solution or Problem?', in M. Cini and A. Bourne (eds) *Palgrave Advances in European Union Studies* (Basingstoke: Palgrave).

Rieger, E. (2000) 'The Common Agricultural Policy', in H. Wallace and W. Wallace (eds) *Policy-making in the European Union* (4th edn) (Oxford: Oxford University Press).

Rosamond, B. (1999) 'Discourses of Globalization and the Social Construction of European Identities' (*Journal of European Public Policy* 6:4, 652–68).

Rosamond, B. (2000) *Theories of European Integration* (Basingstoke: Macmillan).

Ross, G. (1995) *Jacques Delors and European Integration* (Cambridge: Polity Press).

Sandholtz, W. and Zysman, J. (1989) '1992: Re-casting the European Bargain' (*World Politics* 27:4, 95–128).

Sbragia, A. (2000) 'Environmental Policy: Economic Constraints and External Pressures', in H. Wallace and W. Wallace (eds) *Policy-making in the European Union* (4th edn) (Oxford: Oxford University Press).

Scharpf, F. (1999) *Governing in Europe: Effective and Democratic?* (Oxford: Oxford University Press).

Schmitter, P. (1996) 'Imagining the Future of the Euro-polity with the Help of New Concepts', in G. Marks, F. Scharpf, P. Schmitter and W. Streeck (eds) *Governance in the European Union* (London: Sage).

Sherrington, P. (2000) *The Council of Ministers: Political Authority in the European Union* (London: Pinter).

Smith, K. (2004): *The Making of EU Foreign Policy: The Case of Eastern Europe* (2nd edn) (Basingstoke: Palgrave).

Smith, M (2007) 'The European Union and International Poltiical Economy: Trade, Aid and Monetary Policy', in K.E. Jørgensen, M. Pollack and B. Rosamond (eds) *Handbook of European Union Politics* (London: Sage).

Taylor, P. (1983) *The Limits of European Integration* (Beckenham: Croon Helm).

Thielemann, E. (2002) 'The Price of Europeanization: Why European Regional Policy Initiatives are a Mixed Blessing' (*Regional and Federal Studies* 12:1, 43–65).

Uçarer, E. (2006) 'Justice and Home Affairs', in M Cini (ed.) *European Union Politics* (2nd edn) (Oxford: Oxford University Press).

Urwin, D. (1992) *The Community of Europe: A History of European Integration since 1945* (London: Longman).

Wallace, H. (2000) 'The Institutional Setting: Five Variations on a Theme', in H. Wallace and W. Wallace (eds) *Policy-making in the European Union* (4th edn) (Oxford: Oxford University Press).

Wallace, H. and Young, A.R. (2000) 'The Single Market', in H. Wallace and W. Wallace (eds) *Policy-making in the European Union* (4th edn) (Oxford: Oxford University Press).

Waltz, K. (1979) *Theory of International Politics* (Reading, MA: Addison-Wesley).

Warleigh, A. (1998) 'Better the Devil you Know? Synthetic and Confederal Understandings of European Unification' (*West European Politics* 21:3, 1–18).

Warleigh, A. (2000) 'The Hustle: Citizenship Practice, NGOs and Policy Coalitions in the European Union – The Cases of Auto Oil, Drinking Water and Unit Pricing' (*Journal of European Public Policy* 7:2, 229–43).

Warleigh, A. (2002) *Flexible Integration: Which Model for the European Union?* (London: Continuum).

Warleigh, A. (2003) *Democracy in the European Union: Theory, Practice and Reform* (London: Sage).

Warleigh-Lack, A. (2007) ' "The European and the Universal Process"? European Union Studies, New Regionalism and Global Governance', in K.E. Jørgensen, M . Pollack and B. Rosamond (eds) *Handbook of European Union Politics* (London: Sage).

Weigall, D. and Stirk, P. (eds)(1992) *The Origins and Development of the European Community* (Leicester: Leicester University Press).

Weiler, J.H.H. (1991) 'The Transformation of Europe' (*Yale Law Review* 100, 2403–83).

Wessels, W. (1997) 'An Ever Closer Fusion? A Dynamic Macropolitical View on Integration Processes' (*Journal of Common Market Studies* 35:2, 267–99).

Wiener, A. and Diez, T. (eds) (2004) *European Integration Theory* (Oxford: Oxford University Press).

Young, H. (1998) *This Blessed Plot: Britain and Europe from Churchill to Blair* (Basingstoke: Macmillan).

Zielonka, J. (2006) *Europe as Empire: The Nature of the Enlarged European Union* (Oxford: Oxford University Press).

INDEX

Note: Page numbers in *italic* indicate boxed text.